YOUR SOUL PURPOSE

For the ones who feel like they were made for more –
take the first step, and the path will be illuminated.

YOUR SOUL PURPOSE

MANIFEST A LIFE YOU *LOVE*

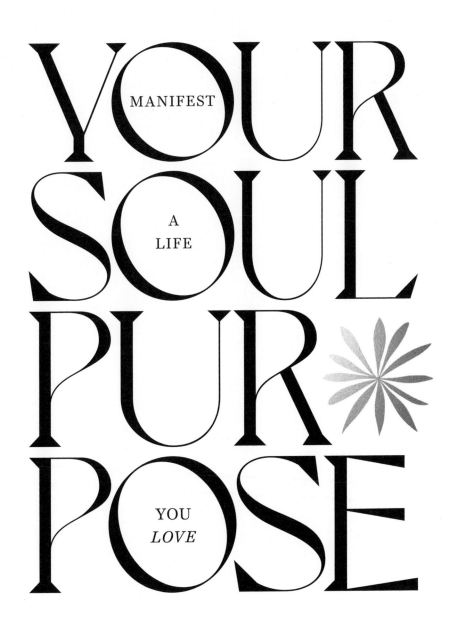

AUBREY DAQUINAG

Hardie Grant

BOOKS

INTRODUCTION

It took a deep-seated surrender for me to feel into my soul's purpose, the first inner spark.

Everything looked great on paper. I had a full-time career in fashion marketing, I was in a long-term relationship with my high school sweetheart, and I was living in a safe and stable home in Australia. The next logical step was to get married and settle down to start a family. While there is nothing wrong with this scenario and many people choose to follow this path, I knew deep down that it wasn't for me at that time. I had other desires. Stepping into the unknown to follow my inner calling was outside of my comfort zone, but I couldn't ignore the whispers anymore. I had to listen to my inner knowing and take a leap of faith.

One of the most courageous things I've ever done was to trust this even when it didn't make sense. Even when it wasn't the easiest option. Even when I didn't know if it was the 'right' choice or if I was messing everything up. When all I could see was the first step illuminated in front of me, I surrendered to the risk of leaving something *good* for the chance of experiencing something *better*.

Before I knew it, I became completely immersed in the nonlinear path of doing what I felt called to do. That unfolding was my initiation into the underworld of my psyche, and so began a journey of peeling away layer upon layer of beliefs, constructs and conditioning, ultimately changing how I viewed the world and, more personally, how I viewed myself. A journey where I invited my intuition to lead the way, making sure to take action in alignment with my greater vision.

I built a successful online travel business that enabled me to explore all corners of the globe and travelled as a full-time travel photographer and creator for my job. I was being paid to create digital content and worldwide campaigns, and even landed an international book deal. But somewhere along the way, I felt like I was missing the true concept of travel – those serendipitous moments, synchronicities and no-plans-that-actually-turn-out-to-be-the-best-plans.

So I ventured out on my own to experience travel from a new perspective and through a different lens – one without deliverables, meetings or schedules. I sold my belongings, put everything into storage, and this time I took only my values, inner compass and sacred practices – the tools that would guide me along the way. I became addicted to this great move with no agenda, and I held on to this tingling feeling, like I was flirting with life.

In my journey, I noticed that too many people were following what everyone else was doing, only to end up unfulfilled because it was not what they truly wanted. They were focusing on the external instead of the intricacies of their inner world, where the driving forces of change were to be found, never taking time to check in with themselves and ask the real questions.

What does it mean to live a life I'm proud of and fulfilled by?

Is how I'm spending my time in alignment with what I value and what makes me happy?

Who would I be if I wasn't afraid to shine my light?

When the industry (and world) shut down in 2020, I became drawn to helping people interact more compassionately with their own thoughts.

The outer-world exploration shifted and evolved to inner-world exploration. This journey placed me deeper into my own purpose – supporting those who were ready to walk on their soul purpose path, to own more of their truth and feel the freedom of true self-expression. Now, through coaching programs, online courses and in-person workshops, I guide leaders and seekers, just like *you*, who want to create and live a life with more purpose, in celebration of their personal power, and offer support and mentorship for those who choose to turn their passion into purpose-driven businesses.

This work is ethereal and transcendent, but most of all it's transformative. It reveals beauty, truth and unshakable self-trust – the kind of self-trust that helps with:

- ◎ *gaining clarity and living a life that feels fulfilling to you*

- ◎ *expressing your authentic voice confidently*

- ◎ *developing unwavering self-belief that it's possible and available for you*

- ◎ *building forward momentum with practical and aligned action steps.*

This work will take you out of living on autopilot, and into becoming who you know you came here to be. So you can live a life that makes you feel fully alive.

WHAT IS SOUL PURPOSE?

We enter into this world wild with innocence, worthy just as we are and free from any social constructs. As children, we follow our natural instincts, say what we mean with no filter, feel into every emotion unapologetically, and never question our impulses or what we deserve as we navigate each moment based on how it feels. We are comfortable being our truest selves.

As life unfolds, we lose touch with that connection. Our views get tainted by disheartening or traumatic experiences, and we start to question if we are, in fact, worthy of receiving love from our relationships, money from doing what we love, or success from our efforts. These beliefs form in our subconscious based on the immediate environment we grow up in. We follow the path of what success is supposed to look like and conform to other people's ideas of what life is supposed to be like, drifting further and further away from what makes us truly feel alive, wild and free. We start to live life on autopilot, and not in alignment with who we are at our core. We lose touch with our soul – the very essence of our being – as societal conditioning creates a version of who we think we have to be in order to live happy and fulfilled lives.

When a life is built in separation from our soul and what we deeply desire, a question always appears: *is this all there is?*

Your soul purpose is firstly to remember the truth of who you are, and then to simply share it with the world. It is the feeling of being lit up from the inside out. The unique expression of *you*.

It is not just about *what* you do, but *why* you do it.

Discovering your soul purpose is a deeply personal journey, and one that is far from linear. It is also empowering: a journey that calls for exploration, self-reflection, experimentation, inspiration, connection, and a willingness to adapt and evolve. It is a process of unlearning as much as it is learning; a humble act of remembering and becoming the most authentic version of yourself at your innermost core. The French have a saying, *voyager à l'intérieur*, which means 'to travel within'. Although this journey is an inner one, you will witness the shifts in your outer reality.

The ironic part is that those who choose to embark on this journey begin by searching outside of themselves rather than looking towards the wisdom found within. This is like a rose asking a peony, 'How do I bloom?' when a rose already has everything it needs to grow, or the sun asking the moon, 'How do I shine?' when the sun already has everything it needs to rise and set exactly on time. Similarly, you and I are part of nature, too. We have come here with everything we need to be and live our purpose.

Once you release the version of yourself you think you should be, you will begin to remember who you truly are.

Your soul purpose is
firstly to remember
the truth of who you
are, and then to simply
share it with the world.
It is the feeling of being
lit up from the inside out.
The unique expression
of being you.

SOUL-ALIGNED SUCCESS

Soul-aligned success is all about being the authentic person you were born to be, and walking on the path of your unique soul purpose. It is a state of fulfilment, like a cup overflowing, because you are in alignment with what matters most to you, doing something that feels much closer and more connected to you. A place where physical possessions do not take precedence over the intangible realm, and inner peace and deep self-love equal the real currency to success. With courage and healing, you can start to become more of your true self and understand the intricacies of how to manifest a life beyond your wildest dreams.

Accessing your soul and stepping into a bolder self-expression of your inner calling comes with the following requirements, which money cannot buy:

- *integrity: the focus on being radically honest with others and, most importantly, yourself*

- *openness: the willingness to invite in new people, experiences and states of mind*

- *gratitude: attuning to what you are thankful and grateful for in this life*

- *trust: learning to surrender to your inner compass and its discoveries with the gift of grace.*

This version of soul-aligned success is defined by no one other than *you*; it is where you can give yourself permission to dream and achieve, but not let the destination rob you of experiencing the journey. It's the sweet spot where being, doing and having are all in harmony.

WHAT TO EXPECT

In this book, you will find a beautiful balance of science, psychology, spirituality and ancient wisdom for the modern day. I will guide you through these pages with practical strategies and share stories from past clients.

Soul self check-ins can be found throughout each chapter – these are specific questions that will help you to reveal answers from within. This is your sacred time to get to know your most true and authentic self. All you need to do is open up honestly, to be greeted by your soul.

There are also **soul purpose practices** at the end of every chapter, which you can use on an ongoing basis to stay connected to your soul purpose.

You may find yourself in any of the four parts of discovery, healing, re-awakening and service. Do not hesitate to turn to the page that you are most drawn to in the moment. In the final chapter, I share a how-to on setting re*soul*utions.

My intention is that with each chapter you will begin to feel more connected to your soul self, your intuition and your deepest knowing. When you rediscover who you truly are, *why* you're here will begin to unfold naturally.

Throughout these pages, I use Universe, God and Source interchangeably to refer to a higher power. Feel free to use or replace these with whatever works best for you. What I am offering are tools for you to use. You are the driver – take what resonates and leave what doesn't. I am here to create the space for you to be guided and reminded.

I invite you to underline, highlight and write your own thoughts within these pages, and to share them with me, *us*.

Before we begin I encourage you to reflect on your starting point. Take some time to journal and answer the following:

What I need more of ...

_____

_____

_____

_____

_____

_____

_____

_____

_____

What I need less of ...

_____

_____

_____

_____

_____

_____

_____

_____

_____

Now that you've identified key elements of what you want in your life, your own journey can begin. I know change can feel scary, but it's through that discomfort that you will experience personal growth.

Travelling solo to far-flung destinations, leaving everything behind to live out in the forest or meditating in the Himalayas is not a prerequisite for discovering your purpose or living a soul-led life. What is a prerequisite, however, are regular check-ins with your true self ... your *soul* self. This can be in the simplest of ways – through breath, the observation of beauty around you, moment-to-moment presence – so long as you filter out the noise, be still, and willingly travel further to the places only *you* can go. All that is needed is your presence to pay attention in the moment, and the courage to curiously follow your inner calling.

Consider this your invitation.

Open heart.

Open mind.

PART ONE

DIS CO

VERY

'Normality is a paved road:
it's comfortable to walk but
no flowers grow on it.'

VINCENT VAN GOGH

CHAPTER — ONE

Inner spark

WHAT LIGHTS YOU UP?

'Is this all there is?'

This was what I wrote in my journal after a long day at work.

Mind you, I didn't hate my job. I had worked my way up in the corporate world of fashion marketing, from a receptionist role at a fashion magazine to assisting on photo shoots, and eventually managing my own clients at a creative agency. The perks of the job included free tickets to music and fashion festivals, and opportunities for creativity and innovation. No two days were ever the same. I thrived on the variety and enjoyed the people I worked with. But, despite all of this, the work I was doing wasn't satisfying.

Have you ever felt this? As though you are meant for more? Not more in the physical sense, but more *you*. More self-expression, more meaning, more trust ... more life.

Maybe you've felt a hint of curiosity towards exploring something more. Your body leaning in for a moment, until a voice driven by fear says, 'You can't do that – you're too old,' or, 'Are you kidding? They'll make fun of you when you fail,' or, 'It's been done. This person is already doing it so well.' And just like that, you shut yourself down.

My inner sparks never went away. All I did was push them to the side. I told myself I would save it for 'some day'.

WHAT IS YOUR INNER SPARK?

Inner sparks light you up from the inside out. They're enthusiastic bits of energy that build when you're passionate about something. Like static electricity, this energy carries information. It is charged with emotion and passion. Your eyes may widen or you may suddenly feel more inclined to pay attention. When you follow your curiosity, you may even find yourself in an uninterrupted presence of flow – forgetting to eat, having no concept of time, hypnotised into a state that feels oh so free.

Most of the time this energy goes unnoticed, or it is dismissed or sadly ignored. It doesn't always make logical sense or feel clear in the present moment, but it makes you feel *something*. Following that something is the key to revealing what you're truly meant to be doing now, or next.

Your inner spark may arrive as an idea to act on, it might become evident in an event or workshop you are intrigued by, or it could reveal itself within a community you feel drawn towards. It can often appear in an activity you find great joy in, when you are engaged and full of wonder, innocence, curiosity and delight.

Through my work in guiding thousands of people towards living a soul-fulfilled life, I've seen people stop following their inner spark because they are waiting for a complete step-by-step plan. They want to know every step, but it's possible to proceed with the first spark illuminated and continuously check in to receive more sparks along the way. Reconnecting with the present moment allows you to recognise your unique inner spark and live in forward motion on your soul purpose path.

Presence is the portal that takes you from here to now.

What is something that lights me up that I haven't given myself the chance to explore?

What do I value?

What are some ways I can honour my values through my actions?

VALUES

To understand your inner sparks, you need to identify your values. Your values make up the essence of your identity and can be best experienced as feelings. They provide inner guidance for navigating your inner sparks and the decisions you make. Your core values support the vision of where you want to go.

Chances are you already know your values or at least have an inkling of what they may be. Often, they are buried in the choices you make when deciding what you spend your time on, what you spend your money on, and who you choose to spend time with. Give yourself time and space, in silence and in solitude, to establish your values. As you evolve into different versions of yourself, values can also change. Being alone will allow you to reflect on and evaluate your current reality, and the conscious changes you need to make to focus your attention where it matters most.

Time is the most valuable currency because you cannot get it back. When you are unintentional with your time it becomes difficult to grasp what you value, and this can make you feel unfulfilled. The modern world is full of distractions and influences that may not feel true to your true self. You may adopt beliefs about what 'success' is, or what life is meant to look like, or what will make you happy. If you don't take time away from distractions and external influences, you can end up going through the motions. When you're intentional with your time, you can choose what is important to you and ensure that your life is filled with meaning, purpose and things that light you up.

Keep your values front of mind when navigating life. They will provide you with fulfilment and make space for the powerful growth and development of your unique vision.

You may find that your inner sparks are linked to activities that you enjoyed as a child. This is no coincidence. It is in our earliest years that we are the clearest, and often the things we enjoyed when we were younger bring us the most joy today. I see this happen a lot with my coaching clients once they let go of the to-do list and make time for the activities they enjoyed as children.

When I was nine, I would often draw faraway places in my journal. 'Where are we going today?' I would ask as I slid open my twelve-pack box of crayons, all of them colourful and perfectly placed beside one another. Then I'd let my scribbles lead the way. I had an 'aha' moment when I finally left my nine-to-five in fashion to follow my inner sparks: I started a blog that led to me becoming a travel photographer, and soon I was creating for brands around the world.

CHARLOTTE
FROM HIGH-ACHIEVING CORPORATE
TO FOLLOWING CHILDLIKE JOY

For many years, Charlotte worked in a corporate role for a high-fashion label in London. She was living the dream her younger self had always imagined: she was a successful, high-achieving woman who thrived under pressure.

After years of this fast-paced lifestyle, she found herself feeling burnt out, and she developed body issues and an eating disorder. She took time off to tend to her healing and wellbeing, and had a moment of realisation in the stillness. Charlotte's reflection revealed a young woman who had achieved so much and yet still felt lost; a woman who was surrounded by people day in, day out, and yet still felt lonely; a woman who was constantly pushing herself and yet wasn't nurturing herself; a woman who, from the outside, looked like she had it all figured out, yet on the inside felt no real meaning or purpose.

Charlotte felt her inner spark longing for something more spacious, and she decided to swap her big-city life for one surrounded by nature. She took a course in holistic health and started practising yoga. Her energy began feeling more vibrant, and she felt herself light up again. Eventually, Charlotte started guiding other women in corporate careers. She led wellbeing programs, workshops and retreats to help them find the balance between their careers and self-care.

Looking back on her journey, Charlotte noticed that the things she had enjoyed doing as a child – such as spending time outdoors in nature – were the same things that brought her happiness as an adult. Her values had guided her decision to change her environment and serve others through her work. She now lives a more spacious and soul-aligned life.

What activities brought me joy as a child?

How can I infuse them into my life today?

EGO VS SOUL

Your ego is what you have learned about yourself from others, your experiences and the society you grew up in. It's the conditioned part of you that keeps you safe from perceived threats. It wants to avoid the negative consequences of going against society's norms and rules. It will create stories to tell you that comfort and familiarity are your safest options. There is a time and place for the ego, but it's best not to let it in the driver's seat.

Your soul, on the other hand, is about expansion. It's the true self that arises from within. Souls are eternal and connected to something far greater than our individual selves. Your soul keeps you alive and wanting more. Our souls make us who we are and connect us all as a whole.

EGO	SOUL
seeks to serve itself	seeks to serve others
seeks outward recognition	seeks inner authenticity
acts on competition	acts on contribution
feels lack	feels abundance
tries to control everything	trusts all is unfolding as it should
separation	union
operates on fear	operates on love
enjoys the prize	enjoys the journey
me	we

What stories does my ego tell me?

What repeating patterns do I notice as a result?

There are no shortcuts or fast passes to living your soul purpose. You can only start from where you are today, fully embracing who you are now and transcending the ego to meet with the soul. As we journey together, you will start to tune in and listen to what your soul has to say.

Ways to simply begin:

1. *Bring your awareness to your inner dialogue.*

2. *Practise presence and observation of the moment right here, right now.*

3. *Take note of your energy levels when you're surrounded by specific people and activities.*

4. *Notice the space between the ego mind and action (or reaction).*

5. *Pay attention to your breath – each inhale and slow exhale.*

6. *Observe your thoughts and emotions when a specific topic comes up in conversation.*

7. *Pay attention to sensations in your body. The body holds truth and will disconnect you from your ego mind.*

8. *Journal honestly about your findings, feelings and realisations.*

9. *Get out into nature to connect with universal sources and see the abundance that exists there.*

10. *Do something you love. Fully immerse yourself in a creative activity you love to bring yourself back to the present moment.*

With anything new or difficult, the instinct to step back and resist is a common response. Remember, the ego's job is to keep you safe. With presence and awareness, you can observe the part of you that is resisting and begin to understand why. Then you can determine what you need to make your way through.

Here are some sneaky ways you might be postponing your soul's calling:

◎ *You're waiting for the right time. (Now is as perfect a time as ever.)*

◎ *You believe you need to get everything in order before you make your move. (You don't.)*

◎ *You're ignoring what your body is trying to communicate. (Listen up.)*

◎ *You've already postponed for too long and now you think it's 'too late'. (It isn't.)*

◎ *You're looking for a sign to start. (This is it.)*

Being in a position to dream about your soul purpose is a privilege. Survival mode fills up most people's mental capacity, while others simply don't want to live their soul purpose, and that's okay too. That's their path. Like all journeys, we must remain in integrity. Understanding that others will choose not to come along for the ride will save you time and energy, as you won't try to convince them. These are not your people. Your people are out there and you will meet them along the way – trust that. Give yourself the grace and luxury of discovery with curiosity and wonder. Tune into your inner guidance. (More on this in Chapter 8.) It will help you feel more connected, and steer you away from following the same patterns with the same people, doing the same things and ignoring the callings of your soul.

Soul Purpose Practice

Think of ways you can experience the joy you felt as a child.

It may be that you loved painting, picking flowers while out in nature or photographing the world around you. Maybe you enjoyed playing dress-up with different outfits, scrapbooking or swimming until sunset. You get the idea.

Carve out time in your calendar to do these things. Consciously incorporate more play in between your rigid schedule and important adult tasks – your body will come to feel your inner sparks, and you will feel flow in ways you may have forgotten, like a return to your inner self.

You might dedicate a whole day on the weekend or do it before or after work during the week. Partners, kids and animals are most welcome, too.

CHAPTER — TWO

Destination of desire

WHERE DO YOU WANT TO GO?

Years ago, I gained clarity on the vision for my dream life. It looked something like this:

- *waking up in a new destination, excited and curious as to what the day would hold*

- *capturing different cultures with my camera and working from cute cafes*

- *seeing payment notifications pop up on my phone and receiving money for doing meaningful work I enjoyed*

- *collaborating with brands and people in alignment with my values and aesthetic*

- *running a thriving creative online business that would give me true freedom and fulfilment.*

I created a vision board to accompany this sensory-led description – a collage of connected photographs of places I would arrive at, both physically and metaphorically, after much hard work and hustle.

Back then, all I knew was that I felt divinely connected to something telling me that the vision for my dream life was already mine. But what I was actually doing was imprinting into my brain my soon-to-be reality.

YOUR DESTINATION

Destination of desire is a simple visioning exercise I do with my clients to help them create their own sensory-led descriptions.

You may already have a destination of desire, whether it's pivoting to a new career path, moving to a new city or country, calling in a romantic partner, or simply living life with greater happiness and inner peace. Deep down, there is always a dream vision that is waiting to come alive and wanting to be experienced. The desire for change is a chance for discovery and experimentation.

When we familiarise our brains with our destinations of desire, we imprint these destinations into the reticular activating system (RAS), a bundle of nerves in the brainstem that filters out unnecessary information so that the important stuff comes through. It's like when you set your sights on a new car and all of a sudden you start seeing that car everywhere – the cars have always been around, but you only register them now that you've signified to your RAS that they're important to you.

When we do this with our desires, our brains start looking for the next steps we can take towards that destination. This opens more doors, which enable us to see more opportunities. Creating this conscious connection allows your brain to filter the world through a new perspective.

Following this guidance will point you in the right direction to achieve soul-aligned success. It's not just about the accumulation of accolades and material gains, or the pursuit of external validation, but the art of living in alignment with your truest essence – the version of you that existed before the world told you who you should be. Your destination is filled with purpose and fulfilment; it's a bold declaration to live authentically. Joy arises when our actions align with our values, when our purposes intertwine with our pursuits, and when we touch the lives of others in meaningful and transformative ways.

You can create a vision board to accompany your destination of desire. You might choose to physically print out pictures and paste them onto a board, or digitally collect images online – as long as your vision board is created with intention. (I like to use images from Pinterest and my own photos.) Make sure you include a photograph of yourself, preferably in your favoured emotional state. The vision board, accompanied with the soul purpose practice, creates the foundation for your attention. Where attention goes, energy flows, and neural connection grows.

SURFACE DESIRE VS SOUL DESIRE

In the modern world, surface desires can manifest as the pursuit of status, wealth, a romantic partner, a dream home or the latest gadget. They can be driven by a fear of missing out or a need to conform to societal expectations. Soul desires, on the other hand, beckon us to dig deeper and listen to the whispers of our hearts and souls. They call us to seek authentic connections, meaningful relationships, creative expressions, and experiences that align with our values, passions and true purposes.

Scientific evidence shows that our thoughts and emotions have vibrational energy, which affects the reality we experience. In the same way, our soul desires tap into the energetic realm of the Universe. What the soul desires most is the frequency of the feeling: the emotional charge, extending beyond physical possessions, linked to every physical manifestation.

Many of us don't know exactly what we're searching for; we just want to feel good. We want to feel like we're on the right path and that what we're doing is the 'right' thing. In our moments of searching, it never occurs to us to stop and listen to the guidance within. Our soul desires are revealed when we sit in solitude and tune into what we really want. Then we have to go a layer deeper to discover *what* these desires signify and *why* they are important to us.

THE WHAT (A DEEPER FREQUENCY)

Let's take a look at money. When we aspire to accrue more money and material wealth, we are brought towards a frequency of abundance. We want to feel secure knowing we can experience life with an overflowing sense of freedom – the freedom to create our own schedules, spend time doing what

SOUL SELF CHECK-IN

What does my destination of desire look like?

we want and feel unlimited in our pursuits. It's not about the money itself – it's about what we will be able to *do* with the money and, most importantly, how that overflowing abundance will make us *feel*.

Similarly, the desire for love goes beyond a quest for a romantic partner's physical presence. While we might crave having someone to kiss and miss, our souls seek something far deeper. The soul longs to experience the frequency of unconditional love, where two souls intertwine in a dance of authentic connection, emotional intimacy, vulnerability and trust.

The pursuit of a dream home is our souls craving more than just brick and mortar. The dream home resonates with a frequency of sanctuary and belonging – a place where we can find solace, express our authentic selves and create lasting memories with loved ones. We seek a harmonious space rooted in serenity, providing refuge from the external chaos of the modern world.

When we chase career success, our souls are yearning for a frequency of fulfilment and purpose. With the energy of aligned work, our passions, talents, skills and values all meet. Each day becomes an expression of our authentic selves, contributing to a greater whole.

When we set our sights on new travel experiences, our souls desire more than just sightseeing. The soul craves the frequency of expansion, adventure and connection with the wider world; we want to be taken out of day-to-day life and encounter new ways of being. The transformative power of travel lies not only in physical movement but also in the expansion of consciousness and the deepening of our connections to the planet and each other.

Ultimately, the material manifestations of our desires are only symbols of the energetic states our souls wish to experience and embody. This doesn't mean we need to disregard physical form and live in complete isolation from the surface – otherwise, how would we know our depths? But it is a chance for us to dive deeper into our inner worlds to see if we are living in alignment with our truths and core values.

THE WHY (YOUR NORTH STAR)

In astronomy, Polaris (also known as the North Star or Pole Star) is the anchor of the northern sky. The northern sky appears to move around Polaris, while the star stays nearly still, and so it is used as a reliable marker to locate the geographic north pole. Just as Polaris glows brightly to show the direction north, your Why illuminates the path towards your soul purpose.

When you clarify your *Why*, or North Star, it will help to:

◎ *create more purpose and meaning behind your actions*

◎ *sustain you through the inevitable tough times*

◎ *make life feel way more fun.*

Without a North Star, we become lost, living on autopilot.

This is not a new concept. In Japan, ikigai provides people with a sense of purpose or reason for living. In ancient Greek philosophy, the concept of eudaimonia, or 'human flourishing', emphasises the importance of living a virtuous life in happiness and good spirit. In ancient Indian philosophy, dharma is to live in accordance with higher truths and find purpose through selfless service to others. In astrology, the North Node or 'destiny' on your

What are the deeper feelings I desire to experience?

natal chart (a snapshot of the position of the planets at the exact time, day and location you were born) represents where you are meant to grow and evolve during this lifetime.

As you start to connect the dots and discern whether your desires are surface-level programming or truly from the soul, you will discover more of the *Why* beneath. Your *Why* will then translate into your mission.

When you are devoted to something bigger than yourself, you will feel mission-driven motivation. This is the highest form of motivation. There is no one pushing you; it is more of an expansive pull towards the vision. You will simply know it is your duty to carry out this purpose during your time here on earth.

BEING, UNTIL YOU BECOME

It's a common scenario for someone to say, 'I won't feel [insert emotion] until I reach my destination.' What they desire feels so close, but it is always one step ahead – within grasp, but not yet actualised in their life. This happens when there is a disassociation: they envision their desire to be over there (in the future), instead of here (present). And what's in the future will – you guessed it – stay in the future.

To bring that future forward, we must merge the vision of our future selves with our current selves and bring the experience of the deeper feelings into our present reality. As humans, we have been gifted the beauty of imagination. We can use our minds to create visions that evoke certain sensations in our bodies as if they were our current reality.

Picture this: you are in the lounge room of your dream home. Take a moment to close your eyes and envision how it looks, sounds and feels. You make your way over to the kitchen and open the door to your fridge. In the fridge, you find a vibrant yellow lemon. You pick it up and squeeze it gently. It is ripe and juicy. You grab a chopping board and knife, cut the lemon in half and ... Chances are, you are already experiencing the sensations in your mouth as you imagine a freshly cut, juicy lemon, without actually having the lemon in physical form.

Through a combination of visualisation and experience, we are able to tap into the feelings associated with the mind–body connection. Anyone who has ever made love knows that part of the pleasure is the anticipation that builds for both the familiar and the unknown. Anyone who has ever gone on a holiday knows that excitement brews from the moment the tickets are booked.

What is an issue or cause I care deeply about? Why?

Finish this sentence: when my destination of desire has already manifested and I am living it as my current reality, I feel ...

This kind of energy is creative: a universal language that we all have the power to harness. We witness it in our own lives through pleasant daydreaming or when we wake from a dream that feels so real it makes us question if it actually happened. Virtual reality takes this a step further: our eyes and ears work the same whether we are in a real world or a virtual one, and the same senses are stimulated to feel certain sensations.

Not only are we able to direct our energy and attention into *what* we want to create, we can also direct it towards *why* we want to create it and *how* it will feel. These feelings (which create our personal vibrations) are experienced in the present moment – through our current selves, we can envision the destination of desire as if it is already our present reality.

What elevates this experience is the detachment from your desire of destination, which can then, for some, raise the question, 'Then what's the point?' The point is to familiarise your mind and body with the feeling: a new frequency, a new perspective. (More on detachment in Chapter 7.) This manifestation creates a magnetic pull towards the present day through the law of attraction: like attracts like, and it's here that we step into the *being* energy.

Being, until you become.

Rather than doing first, we reverse-engineer. We begin with *being* in the energy of our destinations of desire: we imagine we are already there, living and breathing. From here, the next steps for *how* will naturally reveal themselves.

Soul Purpose Practice

From your vision board, bring your destination of desire to life through your senses, and step into the energy of being here.

What details can you see?

_____

_____

What sounds can you hear?

_____

_____

What flavours can you taste?

_____

_____

What scents can you smell?

_____

_____

What emotions can you feel?

_____

_____

CHAPTER — THREE

Signs and synchronicities

WHAT SIGNS ARE YOU OPEN TO RECEIVING?

When I returned to Australia after living in London, I was lost in a state of confusion. I needed a sign.

So, I simply asked for it.

While this most definitely works as a straightforward question, I chose to drop into a twelve-minute meditation. It was an experience I set the mood for. I lit my favourite candle and incense, and kept my journal close by to record what I saw and any sensations I felt. My intention was to remain open and trust whatever sign I received from the Universe. I got centred on my cushion, landed in stillness and was taken on a journey.

This meditation was a guided visualisation that took me through deep breaths and led me down a path. In this visualisation, I entered the front door of a house and was handed a box. Within this box was to be my sign, and whatever came up naturally I was to trust. I opened the box. A leaf lay inside – one that was perfectly symmetrical. My sign.

I'll be honest, I wasn't entirely convinced at first. I still felt sceptical. My heart closed and my mind started to say things like, 'There are leaves everywhere,' and, 'You could go to a park and be surrounded by leaves.' This left no room for synchronicity. While I was aware that it was not just any kind of leaf, I still chose to disregard it.

When have I dismissed a sign that has come my way?

I continued on with my plan to go into the city with my boyfriend at the time. I had just received a package with a new case for my AirPods and I quickly threw it into my tote bag. Later, as I sat down at a cafe and waited to order, I took the case out to look at it properly. It was a clear case with an illustration of the sun and moon. I showed it to my boyfriend and he said, 'It looks like a leaf. A perfectly symmetrical leaf.'

I stared at him in disbelief – it was clearly a sun and moon. I had not mentioned a thing to him about my sign or even told him that I'd asked for one. He was referring to an air bubble that had formed on a corner of the case, creating the shape of, what looked like to him, a perfectly symmetrical leaf. I smiled to myself. As I write this, I'm still smiling.

Receiving that sign reinforced three truths for me.

1. *A higher power is always present.*

2. *We are guided and supported in each and every moment.*

3. *When you ask for a sign, the Universe will communicate back.*

These days, there are still moments when I am caught off guard, like when I am walking along a path and spot a perfectly symmetrical leaf, or when I'm reading a book I've borrowed from the library and come across a tiny dried leaf someone has left in between the pages. These signs often come with a message, and I receive them as a clear exchange of communication: *You are right on time. You are here. Stay present. I am with you.*

The signs, the guidance and the presence are all there. We just need to be open to receive them.

CYNTHIA
FROM POSTCARDS
TO RELEASING THE PRESSURE

Cynthia had a simple and wonderful experience of asking for a sign and then having it delivered with totally unexpected timing. A naturally positive person with a fun-loving outlook on life, Cynthia had found herself in a state of feeling stuck and she couldn't identify a specific reason why. She was travelling solo in Amsterdam at the time, and she decided to use journalling as a prompt to dive deeper and better understand why she felt the way she did. Her thirtieth birthday was fast approaching, and she felt she needed to have more of her life figured out. As she wrote in her journal, she took the opportunity to ask the Universe for a sign to let her know she was on the right path.

She went out to a cafe nearby. As she waited in line to order, hands in her pockets and gaze facing down, she noticed a postcard beside the coffee machine. In big, bold words, it read:

Take your time.
You are exactly where you are meant to be.

It was the sign Cynthia had asked the Universe for. She immediately felt comforted and reassured. There was no pressure to rush. She was exactly where she was meant to be.

When was the last time I experienced a synchronistic moment?

Did I label it as a mere 'coincidence'?

Swiss psychiatrist, psychotherapist and psychologist Carl Jung first used the term 'synchronicity' in a lecture in 1930, and in a 1955 essay he explains meaningful coincidences as akin to working simultaneously in time to meet, that everything and everyone is linked together. Energy is connected.

We can often be too fixed in our ways and consumed by our busy lives to notice these synchronicities, or we do notice them but are quick to dismiss them. We need to widen our view to open ourselves to them. They are significant. They tell us we are on the right path, doing what we are meant to be doing right now.

Even if you are new to the universal language, signs can be transformational. Even if you're sceptical, synchronicities can give you moments of deeper meaning. They provide us with reinforcement. They have the ability to take us from lost and confused to a position of clarity and certainty.

When you start to walk on your soul purpose path, there is no doubt that signs and synchronicities will appear. You will have easy access to reassurance so long as you keep an open mind and heart.

Soul Purpose Practice

Ask for a sign out loud with intent and open awareness.
It can be as straightforward as saying, 'If I'm on the right path,
please show me [insert what you want to be shown here] in the
next twenty-four hours.' Or you might try something more
open like: 'Please send me a clear sign to let me know I'm on
the right path.' Be patient and remain open.

How will you ask for a sign? What will you say?

_____

_____

_____

_____

_____

_____

_____

_____

For a deeper connection, I have created a meditation
for you to ask and receive a sign. You can find it at
www.theloveassembly.com/askforasignmeditation

PART TWO

HE
AL

ING

'If music be the food
of love, play on.'

WILLIAM SHAKESPEARE

CHAPTER — FOUR

Exploring the world, already within

WHAT BURIED STORIES WILL YOU FIND?

In 2015, I was introduced to the spiritual practice of Vipassana by an ex-lover. After what was a year of wild momentary romance, we chose not to continue our relationship. I often kid that he prepared me for the break-up, as the last trip we experienced together was one that brought me closer to my true self.

This trip involved ringing in the new year in Tasmania. The booze, late nights, loud noise and fireworks were becoming stale, and I was open to anything other than a typical celebration. What followed was my first experience of a ten-day residential course, or what's more widely known as a silent retreat, which allowed me to dive deep into and explore my inner world. Although I had no idea what it entailed at the time, it just felt right. No questions were asked, I simply followed what felt good.

We made our way over to a forest in the slopes of Mount Dromedary, about forty minutes by road from Hobart. There is not much else there except tall trees, bushland and native wildlife. We surrendered our phones, cameras and all electronic devices, along with books, pens and journals. The grounds and meditation hall were separated for each gender. We were to accept and abide by the principles, which included no speaking, reading, writing, eye contact, killing (even insects), sexual play or self-pleasure. We had free will to leave whenever we wished; however, if that was the choice, we would be unable to return.

As your meditation practice deepens, there comes a restructuring of your inner world: your sense of self and how you view the world as it takes place.

Vipassana translates to 'insight', meaning to 'see things as they really are'. It is one of India's most ancient techniques of meditation and focuses on observing the impermanence of the present moment without judgement, and more deeply, on uncovering the true nature of reality. As the practice deepens, there comes a restructuring of your inner world: your sense of self and how you view the world as it takes place. This reflection and questioning of existence brings you into wholeness and universal oneness.

It is a sacred, transformative practice that I've kept close while travelling solo, knowing that I am never truly alone and always connected to something far greater than myself. A practice that has helped me move through times of hurt, suffering, grief, fear and turmoil with more grace. A practice that I have since dived deeper into studying and integrating, knowing how much clarity, strength, happiness and inner peace it brings me. A practice I have willingly led others through when the world was forced into lockdown, knowing how much clarity, strength, happiness and inner peace it would bring them. A practice that has become part of my own mission, which I wholeheartedly invite you to do, to bring you closer to your true essence and live from this space.

What are some beliefs I have told myself that may be holding me back?

SELF-CONCEPT

Everything we want in life requires an identity shift. Money and wealth. A loving relationship. A healthy, functioning body. Career and business success. It all comes down to our self-concept.

Self-concept is who we believe we are. This is constructed from what we believe to be true about the world, and ourselves. It is our dominant 'I am' statements. You might catch yourself saying, 'I'm just the kind of person to ...' or 'That's me'. These statements reveal clues as to how we currently view ourselves, and what we believe about ourselves is what we manifest.

Most people go about making change from the outside in. They look at their actions and behaviours and try to form new habits. This is a great starting point but what can often come up is resistance. This resistance can show up in the form of emotions (e.g. fears that stop us from taking action and moving forward), excuses (e.g. 'I don't have X, therefore I can't do Y') and distractions (e.g. choosing to binge on a TV series instead of taking action towards a dream/goal). A study published in the *Journal of Clinical Psychology* found that only 46 per cent of people who make New Year's resolutions are successful. More than half the people who set a goal for the new year fail by the second month in.

The most potent change comes from the inside out. The less we resist, the more we become. The less we doubt ourselves, the stronger our belief, which leads to more empowering thoughts. The fewer the excuses as to why something won't work out, the more our thoughts will reflect all the reasons why it will. The fewer the distractions that keep us feeling stuck, the more we can focus on what lights us up and makes us feel alive.

What will end up happening is that we will start taking more aligned actions with less resistance and more confidence because we're doing it from a foundation of stronger self-belief. This self-belief is formed from the stories we tell ourselves, and what we believe to be true about ourselves and the world.

BELIEFS: *the stories we tell ourselves, what we believe to be true about ourselves and the world*

THOUGHTS: *what we think*

EMOTIONS: *what we feel*

BEHAVIOUR: *the actions we take*

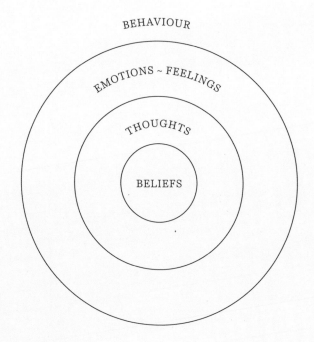

While some of us may feel afraid to start due to the fear of failure, some of us are afraid to start because of the complete opposite – the fear of success. While success is generally seen as desirable, there are people who fear reaching their full potential and being the best version of themselves. Wild, right? This fear is often based on the potential outcomes and consequences that success will bring.

Some pre-conceived notions of success include:

- *being a target of attack: the fear of criticism and potential bad things that will happen to us or loved ones if we are successful or in the spotlight*

- *being lonely: the fear of having no time for those close to us, and worrying about rejection from our loved ones*

- *being seen as a 'show-off': the fear of being labelled as obnoxious, full of yourself or boastful for shining your light.*

While there is truth in being open to greater criticism, outgrowing old relationships that don't align, and people who may judge, the preconceived notions stop any kind of progress. Deep down there's a belief that contributes to self-sabotaging behaviour. Most of the time, we aren't consciously aware of our fear of success, but it can cause people to shrink without even having the chance to shine a sliver of their light.

This traces back to our core beliefs and self-concept. When the work is done from the inside out, we start to operate from a sense of personal power as opposed to force.

Let's be real, most of the time fear may well and truly still be present (welcome to being human), but having courage allows us to move forward despite it being by our side. We need to learn not to let it hold us back. This links back to the 'being' energy I tapped into earlier: *being, until you become.*

Here are some common self-beliefs that may show up in different areas of your life.

HEALTH
'It's too difficult to make any real impact on my health.'

How it can show up: believing health and wellness are out of your control; eating poorly; becoming sick or ill; avoiding exercise; not even trying because it seems pointless.

LOVE AND RELATIONSHIPS
'My needs are shameful or invalid.'

How it can show up: not opening up and being honest with your partner; not expressing vulnerability or communicating needs in a relationship due to the fear of rejection.

CAREER AND BUSINESS SUCCESS
'I'm not experienced/qualified enough.'

How it can show up: enrolling in every course to feel qualified; finding it difficult to trust in your own decision-making; watering down your true expression to fit in; not sharing your opinions; capping the amount of joy or success or abundance you are 'allowed'; not taking action, stalling or never getting started on any ideas.

MONEY
'Money is evil.'

How it can show up: believing that it's bad to want more money and therefore labelling yourself a 'bad person'; not asking for a raise at work; undercharging for your products or services; blocking the flow of receiving money; not meeting your earning potential.

SOUL SELF CHECK-IN

What resistance am I currently feeling?

CLARA
FROM MONEY MINDSET BLOCKS TO BREAKING UPPER LIMITS

Clara had already seen success in her online business as a health and wellness practitioner, but noticed her growth and monthly revenue had plateaued. The reason she had gone into online business was so she could earn an unlimited amount in her purpose-driven work. Every part of her wanted the business to grow, but she was feeling a subtle resistance and didn't know why. She was determined to break free from her own limiting beliefs, and we started working together to get to the root of her beliefs about money that might potentially be holding her back.

Reflecting on her past, we were able to pinpoint a core belief she had about money and success that she wasn't consciously aware of but which was creating resistance to moving forward. For Clara, more money meant more responsibility. She felt she was too young to handle the responsibility of expanding and scaling the business. So when momentum in the business started to build, she would slow it down to a level she was comfortable with. Gay Hendricks, an American psychologist and author, calls this the 'upper limit': a self-imposed barrier to your success created by fear and a scarcity mindset.

Clara's deep-rooted fear of success stemmed from her childhood upbringing. She had witnessed her mother working a lot, which led to relationship issues with her father. This fuelled Clara's fears about money as well as her own relationship.

Healing the deep wounds not only changed her money mindset but also the way she ran her business. Through our work together, we were able to reprogram Clara's subconscious narratives to break through those limitations and allow for her nervous system to feel safe with expansion instead of automatically resorting to a fight, flight or freeze response. Clara learned to show up more confidently in her vision and self-concept, and has now expanded her team of assistant coaches, allowing her to delegate tasks and free up her own time.

INNER CHILD HEALING

Peeking into our past is common in therapy. As we explore the world already within, the paths of inner child healing and shadow work can intersect, revealing deeper parts of ourselves that we may have ignored, neglected or suppressed. Scepticism can be a shadow too, providing an invitation for us to lean in more and trust. We all have an inner child within us. The healing takes place for our younger selves, who were never quite loved in the right way or the way we needed as children, which created inner child wounds. Parents or carers may also carry their own inner child wounds. When we embrace our own wounded inner child, it goes beyond just us – the healing work is generational. Your current story is no one's fault and you can't change the past. What you can do is bring awareness to the present and consciously choose to switch the lens you're currently viewing it through, to one that does support you. One that does serve you. One that does empower you.

Caring for and loving this wounded inner child is creating the safe and secure inner and outer environments that our younger selves needed. It's a chance for us to explore our true feelings and the parts of ourselves that may have been dismissed or rejected, or labelled as 'inappropriate' or 'too much' by others. By embracing and nurturing our inner child while exploring and integrating our shadow, we can cultivate a sense of wholeness, authenticity and emotional wellbeing in our lives. We can begin to acknowledge and heal any unresolved emotions or traumas from our past and integrate those parts of ourselves that we may have pushed away or denied. We can then gain insight into the underlying causes of our behaviours to break free from the repetitive patterns that hold us back from living a fulfilled and authentic life, and give ourselves the permission to flourish through a process of playful discovery and compassionate healing.

Soul Purpose Practice

Carry a journal and write down every time you feel any form of resistance.

Pay attention to the particular patterns of the thought and ask yourself: *Is this true? Is this helpful? Where did it stem from?*

Then replace the thought by reframing it from a different perspective – one that is true and helpful.

What patterns of thought do you experience frequently? How might you reframe them?

_____

_____

_____

_____

_____

_____

_____

_____

_____

CHAPTER — FIVE

Subconscious shifts

WHAT PERSPECTIVES CAN YOU SHIFT TO TRANSFORM?

Imagine you are looking through the lens of a kaleidoscope. Through its mirrors, you see beautiful symmetrical patterns, vibrantly coloured beads and fragments of glass reflecting back at you. Your mind is just like a kaleidoscope. The more you shift, the more your view changes. Pieces tumble together to create new patterns, new perspectives.

We all have our own unique kaleidoscope. Our individual perceptions are shaped through this particular lens. What is reflected back to you is formed by the interdependent fragments from your past. What you see are the beliefs and ideals from your parents, caretakers, teachers, culture and collective consciousness, that have been passed down from generations before, creating a picture of who you think you are. These reflections are how you make sense of life. You put meaning into these pieces and they form your world.

These tiny beads and fragments of glass create a picture of what life should look like, be like and feel like. What is accepted as success. What you have learned about who the world wants you to be. You don't believe it because it's true, it's true because you believe it. But you are not the beads or the fragments of glass.

You are the one looking into the lens through which all of life has the chance to be observed.

To unbind from the social conditioning of others, you simply need to take a step back from what you are seeing, to where you are seeing it from. To view yourself not as your thoughts, but to become aware of yourself thinking the thoughts that come and go, as well as others that may be on repeat. To not become your emotions, but to simply notice the feelings your emotions evoke within your body. To not even be so fixated on your body, as you are simply a soul who views life through this physical vessel here on earth. Like a radio frequency, people can be tuned to see differently. Once you focus on a vision, you will start to see more of what you've imprinted into your reticular activating system and start experiencing it as your new normal.

Awareness is only the beginning. Acknowledgement, the next step. The acceptance to make peace with the experiences that elicit a certain emotion is the precise moment when the healing process begins. To touch with love that which was previously approached with fear. Maybe you don't like to refer to it as healing because it makes you feel broken. But healing can be done while you are already whole. Don't let the ways of the world convince you otherwise.

From this healing, you can start to trace back your past experiences and explore a whole new world, one that's already within. This deep inner work is the real work, and it is here that you will start to experience the shifts in your outer reality as you work, from the inside out.

THE SUBCONSCIOUS MIND

Our subconscious makes up over 90 per cent of our mind. Whenever
I share this piece of information, I like to take a dramatic pause.
Because if there's one thing this is saying, it's that our subconscious is
basically running the show in our lives. This part of the mind is not fully
aware but it influences all of our actions and feelings. For example, we
don't have to think about the simple yet life-inducing act of breathing,
it just happens subconsciously. However, we can become consciously
aware of how to change and control our breath and its pattern. With each
deep inhale, we allow more oxygen into our body and signal to our brain to
wind down. With every elongated exhale, we slow down and ease tension,
stress and anxiousness. This deep conscious abdominal breathing from
the diaphragm activates our parasympathetic nervous system. This takes
us out of the fight-or-flight stress response and into the rest-and-digest
mode, to slow down our heart rate and expand our sense of calm.

Other subconscious behaviours include skills that we have learned like
driving a vehicle or playing an instrument. As we practise with repetition,
the brain slowly rewires to make the neural connections for that particular
skill a little bit stronger. This is due to the brain's plasticity. Our brains are
incredible forces of nature, and after time the skill becomes hardwired into
the subconscious so we can drive without having to concentrate too hard,
or even play the piano or guitar with our eyes closed.

Like a computer hard drive, the subconscious mind is a databank. It's not in
focal awareness but it stores every piece of information, such as our beliefs,
experiences, memories, skills – everything we have seen, done or thought.

What is a memory in my subconscious that is not directly in focus every day?

How do I feel about it?

Say you're having lunch with some old friends and the conversation leads to talking about a party from back in the day. You might suddenly recall what you were wearing (maybe even question it too!), what songs were playing, who was there, and maybe even the words exchanged between you and your crush. Your own little vignette of a past experience. This memory is not directly in focus every day, but it's stored in your subconscious and comes into your awareness when prompted. The moments we experienced in childhood and adolescence contribute to the creation of our subconscious beliefs.

We create our own unique model of the world based on our personal experiences. At any given moment, our brain is being flooded with millions of bits of information happening around us, but we are consciously only aware of a small portion of them. Our conscious mind either deletes, distorts or generalises those bits of information, to prevent us from sensory overload, functionally breaking down or being overwhelmed. As we have evolved as humans, these three internal filters have enhanced our survival.

Let's unpack them a little further.

DELETE

Sometimes we pay selective attention to certain aspects of our experiences and the brain will delete bits of information that it feels are not relevant to us. A basic example of this is when we focus on all of the things going wrong in our lives, encouraging the brain to fixate on seeing the bad in every situation. But if we focus on what is going well, the brain will fixate on the good. This is why incorporating a gratitude practice can be powerful.

DISTORT

Our interpretations of past experiences are based on our own subjective view of reality, not an objective view of reality. Distortion happens when we misrepresent our experiences. We attach meaning to events through our limited view and set of beliefs. For example, there might have been a time you thought a crush wasn't interested because they spoke so little to you, but in reality perhaps the feelings were reciprocated but they were just a little shy.

GENERALISE

Generalisation happens when we take one aspect of our experience and apply it across multiple or all of our experiences. While this can be helpful at times to recognise patterns from our past experiences, it might not always move you forward. Let's say you had an experience when you were seven years old where you had to make a speech in front of the class. You forgot the words and the rest of the class laughed, which made you feel embarrassed. Now, when you have to speak up, you experience the same feelings. What your brain has done is generalise events like this (speaking up) as embarrassing, rather than an empowering chance to share your voice.

Unpack the programming: what past experience could this resistance have come from?

Explore what happened.

IDENTIFYING YOUR SUBCONSCIOUS BELIEFS

Most of our subconscious beliefs are programmed into us between the ages of zero and seven years old. This is when our brains are in an open and receptive state, learning from the environment around us. Our minds become imprinted with stories and meaning from what we are taught to believe from our caretakers and lived experiences. These self-narratives and patterns are stored deep in our subconscious mind and they now run the show in our day-to-day life. Some of these stories and patterns may work in our favour, others not so much. The great news is that we can rewrite the stories, reprogram our subconscious and shift into a new paradigm with beliefs and narratives that better serve us.

We have evolved as human beings in so many ways, yet our physical responses to stress, change or non-life-threatening risk are still governed by our ancient instincts. Luckily in today's modern world, most of us don't usually face these fight-or-flight survival situations, but the instincts that once protected us in the wild can now cause real interference with our ability to instigate wanted change.

Within our brains, there are three deep regions.

1. *Amygdala: The amygdala's main job is to look out for life-threatening situations. It tries to protect us at all costs. All of the information that travels to our brain from our five senses passes through the amygdala. If it detects something which it perceives as life-threatening, it triggers the stress response, also known as the fight, flight or freeze response. The body then starts to flood with the stress hormones adrenaline and cortisol, and these in turn create physiological responses such an increased heart rate, sweaty palms, and rapid and shallow breathing.*

While the amygdala has good intentions, it can often mistake stress for
real-life threats or survival and stops the prefrontal cortex from getting
the information it needs to help us make good choices.

2. *Prefrontal cortex (PFC): The prefrontal cortex intelligently regulates our*
   thoughts, actions and emotions. It is a part of our brain that significantly
   contributes to planning, decision-making, working memory, social
   behaviours, personality development and focusing one's attention.
   It sends and retrieves memories to and from the hippocampus.

3. *Hippocampus: The hippocampus is like a librarian. It is the deep part*
   of the brain that stores and recalls memories and has a major role
   in learning. When the amygdala is upset or in a triggered state, the
   hippocampus can't store memories or properly bring them to mind.

The rate at which our lives are changing has meant that our brains have not
kept pace. Relationship problems, money worries, work issues and even
differences of opinion can be perceived as 'life threats'. The amygdala is
constantly misinterpreting the information that it receives, triggering our
stress responses unnecessarily.

By appealing to our ancestral programming and practising brain–heart
coherence – aligning our thoughts with our actions and intentions – we
can mindfully navigate these old systems and consciously create new
programming with full presence and self-awareness. In time, our bodies
will learn to decipher the difference between actual threats and the exciting
stress of taking risks. We will be able to take control over any irrational
emotional reactions and bring the amygdala to a calm state. Once the
amygdala is in a calm state, it can give the prefrontal cortex what it needs.

SUBCONSCIOUS REPROGRAMMING

In my masterclasses, we make a conscious effort to approach the reprogramming process with detached energy; one that is focused on curiosity and compassion rather than spite and blame. Beginning with this intention and believing that everyone did the best they could with what they had at the time sets the tone for a higher success rate.

As we get to the root cause and discover deep truths within, we can begin to create transformative inner shifts by reprogramming our current set of beliefs and narratives to more empowering ones. This can happen through simple everyday shifts such as calling out your beliefs on the spot through to an ongoing meditation practice where you can sit, be present with the emotion, and hold space for yourself to just feel.

We have five main brainwave states. The best time for our minds to go through the reprogramming process is either first thing in the morning or right before we go to sleep. This is when our brain waves are shifting into Theta, the realm of the subconscious that is most open and receptive to suggestibility. In these moments of inner focus, we are able to plant the words, stories, scenarios and narratives that will best serve us. Perception is the reality we experience. Through mental rehearsal and repeatedly imagining performing an action or scenario, the circuits in our brains can reorganise themselves to reflect our intentions. There are brain scans that show that the structure of the brain changes after only three months of a consistent daily meditation practice. The brain doesn't distinguish between the internal world of the mind and the external environment. It thinks it is the same thing and the brain will function as if the experience has already happened.

DELTA	Deep sleep
THETA	Light sleep, fatigue, meditation, internal focus
ALPHA	Relaxation, calm state
BETA	During most activities while awake, alert
GAMMA	Focused and aware, active mind

Reprogramming will take time because these are beliefs or stories that we have held on to since our early years. This is why repetition is key. As we learn new things, our brain is constantly being rewired. But there are times when we forget our new learnings because the rewiring is only temporary. Each time we repeat a new pattern, the neural pathway becomes a little bit stronger and it eventually becomes second nature. So be patient and show yourself some compassion.

Deep inhale for five seconds and exhale for another five seconds. Set the intention by saying quietly to yourself or out loud, 'I give patience and compassion to myself and all involved throughout this process.'

Soul Purpose Practice

Shift the narratives that no longer serve you
by creating new empowering beliefs.

1. Write these new beliefs down.
Use words that resonate with you.

_____

_____

_____

_____

_____

_____

2. Record them on a voice recorder or on your smartphone.
(Add some binaural beats if you're feeling fancy.)

3. Repeat them daily out loud or by listening to
the recording in the morning and/or evening.

CHAPTER — SIX

Emotional alchemy

HOW DEEP ARE YOU WILLING TO FEEL, TO HEAL?

I used to think that being an empath was a curse.

As an empath, you are able to feel every emotion deeply, mine or yours. That means being a witness to the highs of joy and elation just as intensely as the lows of sadness and misery. As a highly sensitive person (HSP), observation becomes the solution when having to navigate the energies all around you.

Believing that being an empath was a curse was a self-narrative that was subconsciously on loop for me. It made me hide my natural gifts and ignore my intuitive skill. It created this belief that I was 'too much' while simultaneously 'never enough' – a paradox that left me feeling stuck and unable to move forward. But big things can happen with even the smallest perspective shift. The things you once thought were a curse can end up being your biggest superpower.

The word 'emotion' is derived from the Latin *emotere*, which literally means 'energy in motion'. In ancient Chinese medicine it's called *chi* or *qi*, in yoga it's called *shakti*, in the West it's called energy. While it goes by many different names, one thing is common to all – it's limitless. Emotions are a universal language, emitting a range of different frequencies and determining our personal vibration. Emotions are what bring colour to our life experiences. They are the vibrancy in each of our vignettes when we look back in reflection or contemplation. It is here that a whole colour palette awaits; without them, we'd be living in black-and-white worlds.

In *Power vs Force*, David R Hawkins understands the common emotions as emitting high or low vibrations on an emotional scale. As we work our way up the scale, there is love, peace, gratitude and enlightenment. These emotions feel expansive, light-filled and hold a sense of ease. Singing and dancing at a festival is associated with feeling a 'high vibe'. The emotions on the lower frequency, such as shame and guilt, are constrictive and sticky. Jealousy of someone's success is considered a 'low vibe'. The neutrality of courage and acceptance are located in the middle of the emotional scale. The majority of people don't want to stay too long in moments of sadness or misery because it is uncomfortable; however, a simple reframe can help shift our entire perspective. It's not the emotion that's the problem – it's the relationship we choose to have with it.

Research from a Harvard brain scientist has shown that it only takes ninety seconds for the chemical process of an emotion to move through the body. Any remaining emotional response afterwards is how the individual has decided to react to it. Denying an emotion the opportunity to move through the body by suppressing or ignoring it is not courageous. Though we've been led to believe the opposite, to honour emotion takes strength.

SOUL SELF CHECK-IN

If [insert emotion here, e.g. fear] were to speak to me, what would it say?

It takes courage and bravery to allow the full spectrum of emotions to be seen, felt and heard. The most courageous act is to be able to go into the depths of darkness, feel the pain and still choose to live with your heart fully open.

This is why we feel so much better after a good cry. Or why attending a boxing class can be a great stress relief to let out our frustrations. The healthier the outlet, the more we can allow our minds and bodies to heal by feeling. It takes courage and bravery to allow the full spectrum of emotions to be seen, felt and heard. The most courageous act is to be able to go into the depths of darkness, feel the pain and still choose to live with your heart fully open. We won't be able to heal what we're not willing to reveal and feel. Gratitude allows space for all emotions to exist. It is the alchemisation of all emotions.

This emotional alchemy invites and engages with curiosity. It allows all parts of our raw and real experiences to be seen, felt and heard without the need for judgement, or the need to crack a joke to appear unfazed to others or lighten the mood. While humour is a great way to make light of situations, it can also be a defence mechanism; we can sometimes use it to mask the fear of going deeper because we're afraid of what we'll actually have to face.

All parts are welcome. The hurt, the shame, the embarrassment – they provide us with valuable information that can be transformed to work for us instead of against us, by using the energy of the emotion to fuel positive action.

When you fear no feeling, you are free.

EMOTIONS AS MESSENGERS

Our subconscious is the most open and vulnerable in childhood. Memories captured during these earlier years hold a distorted view of how we see the world and how we see ourselves. We all have narratives that we cling to that dictate our behaviours, whether we are aware of them or not. Later in life, a person, situation or event might trigger a memory stored in our subconscious of a positive or negative experience, releasing chemicals or hormones that influence our emotions. The physiological state produced is subconsciously linked to a memory.

Just as joy, excitement and pleasure are part of life, challenges, frustrations and pains are all inevitably involved too. Many people choose to suppress the latter because they are difficult, but what we need to do is acknowledge the value in them. To recognise and embrace all emotions that come with pain and pleasure, tragedies and miracles, shadow and light, we hold duality. We even play witness to feeling multiple emotions at once. From a neutral stance, we can then try to understand them at a deeper level and listen to the messages of value they are attempting to deliver.

The following are examples of some common emotional states we might encounter when we choose to follow the inner callings of our soul purpose. When we can recognise our responses to these emotions, we are able to become less defensive and improve our relationship with them. We can then choose for each emotion to meet a state that will support us in moving forward.

Do I have a tendency to welcome or suppress my emotions?

FEAR, MEET CURIOSITY

'Are you sure about this? We're safe staying right here.'

Fear is a natural, primitive emotion that arises with the threat of harm – physical, emotional or psychological; real or imagined. People fear things they don't understand. I encourage you to get familiar with fear. Take it out for dates, dance with it, laugh, cry and allow yourself to get to know it intimately so you can understand how it shows up in your body. Then learn to respond, rather than react.

Here's what I've gathered to be true from my own fear: all it wants is for me to hear it out and to be held in the moment. So I soften my body, quieten my mind, listen to the guidance within and move forward from my hips and heart space. I become less guarded and more available, showing it love and compassion.

Fear lives in the mind. Your mind can play tricks in an attempt to keep you safe – that's its job. But your soul is here for growth and expansion. Soul guides you to see through the lens of curiosity, enthusiastically experimenting with every step like a child trying something for the first time, with no attachment to the outcome, only the purpose of practising light-hearted play. Curiosity avoids assumptions and asks empowering questions in order to understand.

Try this:
I have named my fear ...
The story it's telling me is ...
When I believe this story I react by ...
When I let go of this story I can make a choice to feel curious by ...

What do I fear?

How would it look through the lens of curiosity?

SELF-DOUBT, MEET WORTHY

'Who do you think you are?'

Self-doubt is similar to fear, but sassier. In 1978, American psychologists
Pauline Clance and Dr Suzanne Imes first coined the term 'imposter
syndrome' to describe the psychological patterns around thoughts of being
undeserving and doubtful of one's achievements and accolades, which can
often lead to self-sabotaging behaviour. Although self-doubt may seem like
it knows what it's talking about (and does it convincingly well sometimes),
it operates in protection mode from a hurt once experienced, and never
feels worthy of what it actually is. Focus on the evidence and the self-doubt
will start to feel worthy of the wins.

Try this:
I have named my self-doubt ...
The story it's telling me is ...
When I believe this story I react by ...
When I let go of this story I can make a choice to feel worthy by ...

SOUL SELF CHECK-IN

What does worthiness feel like in my body?

ANGER, MEET INNER PEACE

'What the f*ck was that?!'

Anger knows how to make an entrance. But anger is normally the after-effect of a more vulnerable emotion. When we experience fear, sadness or a sense of loss, it can be uncomfortable and difficult to accept, and this can subconsciously shift into anger. Traumatic events also keep emotions stored and locked up tight, and everyday triggers show up as reminders of these memories that keep us anchored in the past and feeling anger. Investigating this anger can uncover deeper messages. Perhaps an emotional need is not being met, boundaries have been crossed, a core value has been compromised, or an old wound needs some love, attention and healing.

The traditional practice of reconciliation and forgiveness in Hawaii is called Hoʻoponopono. It involves four humble phrases that ask for forgiveness and express gratitude and love in light of healing and transforming relationships within oneself and others: *'I'm sorry. Please forgive me. Thank you. I love you.'* With regular practice, reciting these four simple phrases can help to restore inner peace and self-love at the times when we need it most. This forgiveness is healing – for the self and others.

Try this:
I have named my anger ...
The story it's telling me is ...
When I believe this story I react by ...
When I let go of this story I can make a choice to feel inner peace by ...

How can I practise forgiveness and compassion for myself or another?

ENVY, MEET APPRECIATION

'Who do they think they are?'

Envy is often a combination of admiration, irritation and discontent –
admiration or irritation towards someone externally, and discontent
towards something internally. Envy can highlight parts within ourselves
that we have not given ourselves the opportunity to express or share.
The alchemisation begins by diving deeper to get to the root of the internal
discontent. Once we have an awareness of what it is we are passionate or
care deeply about, we need to show appreciation of the fact that we have
revealed the most important parts of ourselves which we desire to express
and share.

Try this:
I have named my envy …
The story it's telling me is …
When I believe this story I react by …
When I let go of this story I can make a choice to feel appreciation by …

Who do I envy?

What do they do that I haven't given myself the opportunity to do?

GRIEF, MEET ACCEPTANCE

'I'm sorry.'

Grief is a valid emotional experience that no two people can experience or express in the same way. We can also hold on to other people's pain and get so locked up in feeling other people's loss that we sometimes don't have enough space to feel our own. Alchemising grief means giving up control and surrendering to find a way to dance together, to cry together, to break, scream and hurt together, in order to hold the light towards the wounds so that we can also heal together. Grief calls for a strong support network. We are social beings and we can often find ourselves in holes too deep to climb out of alone. Strength is also accepting that you need help and asking for it. Whether you believe in reincarnation or mourn the loss of your past self as you emerge into a new you, grief can take many forms. As you become more connected to the intuitive guidance within, you might experience an undoing of the behaviours and identity you clung to before deciding to follow your soul purpose path.

Try this:
I have named my grief ...
The story it's telling me is ...
When I believe this story I react by ...
When I let go of this story I can make a choice to feel acceptance by ...

SOUL SELF CHECK-IN

As I lean into acceptance, how can I surrender some more?

PERFECTIONISM, MEET GOOD ENOUGH

'That's not good enough.'

Perfectionism is the nemesis of progress. It is a primary block that keeps us from attending to our creative impulses and experimenting, the belief that things should always be better, and what we have is never enough. Healthy perfectionists work towards high goals and standards; maladaptive perfectionists, however, set extremely unrealistic expectations, which can never be met.

This feeling of perfectionism is buried deep beneath the subconscious stories that have told us we will never be 'enough'. It is fear, self-doubt, obsessive thinking and reassurance-seeking all bundled into one, rooted in the belief that our self-worth is based solely on our achievements. To overcome the paralysis of perfectionism, we need to make peace with 'good enough', to know that we are innately worthy as we are.

Try this:
I have named my perfectionism ...
The story it's telling me is ...
When I believe this story I react by ...
When I let go of this story I can make a choice to feel good enough by ...

How have I progressed in the last year?

What are some ways I can celebrate my growth?

CARMEN
FROM HIGH EXPECTATIONS
TO A HEALTHY DOSE OF FUN

Carmen enjoyed her day job but something inside her still felt unfulfilled. A part of her felt like she had lost herself and that she was living the life that others expected of her. Often, she would find herself going into spirals of self-doubt, negative self-talk and self-criticism. She would pick up momentum with her true passion of being a digital artist but noticed herself pulling back once she started to see traction and success. She knew that the only thing blocking her from creating the life of her dreams was herself and it was time to get out of her own way – 'If I don't invest in myself now and take my life where I want it to go, then when will I?'

Within three weeks of working together, we had already had big breakthroughs. Carmen had been raised by a single mother, and she felt pressure to be practical in her career choices and to go down a sensible path. By recognising when hypercriticism and perfectionism showed up in her mind and body, she was able to release the energetic blocks and subconscious beliefs that were holding her back.

Her dedication to the inner work organically led to inspired aligned action. By the end of the program, she went from being stuck in a spiral of self-doubt and people-pleasing, to possessing unshakable self-belief and being at peace with her story. She tuned in to her inner spark, let go of the pressure of expectations and leaned into having more fun. She came to understand that fun wasn't frivolous; it was an extremely important part of mental wellbeing. This led her to share her illustrations and art online, resulting in more collaborations and building a community. Most importantly, she felt fulfilled – 'full in life, full in joy, full in creativity, and fully expressing my truth'.

EMOTIONS IN THE BODY

Our bodies hold and produce sensations that reveal how we're truly feeling on a subconscious level. We store emotions in the body and, as revealed by the evolving neuroscience of trauma research on the body in *The Body Keeps the Score* by Bessel van der Kolk, new treatments in body-oriented therapies and traditional mind–body practices make it possible for sufferers of traumatic stress to reclaim their lives.

In a series of experiments done at Harvard Business School, psychologist Alison Wood Brooks revealed how the shift from anxiousness to excitement is much easier to achieve than trying to calm down. Anxiety and excitement feel strikingly similar in sensation – the same physiological reaction of adrenaline makes its way through the body in both states. The difference is in how our mind interprets the experience along with the story we attach to it. Anxiety normally hatches a story around resistance, thinking things will go wrong, imagining the worst-case scenario, making fools of ourselves and people laughing at us. In contrast, while the physiological response is the same, excitement's story looks forward to the future, imagining how all the things will go well, and welcomes it with open arms. So instead of changing the basic physiology, what can be more easily achieved is changing the story around it. If we tell ourselves, 'I'm so nervous,' our minds correlate it to our bodies and more stress hormones will be produced. Telling ourselves 'I'm so excited' repeatedly recalibrates old programming, and things that once induced anxiousness can actually start to have new narratives linked to them.

By activating our
bodies in natural and
spontaneous ways,
our brains are taught to
welcome new ideas,
thoughts and patterns
of behaviour.

RELEASING STAGNANT ENERGY

Emotions are an integral part of our human experience and how we choose to feel shapes everyday moments, whether big or small. Although the chemicals that flow from our emotions are inevitable, we are in control of how we respond. Emotions that we may have suppressed or that arise within situations that we feel are no longer serving us can remain as stuck or stagnant energy that gets trapped in our bodies. We can start to release these through movement and connecting to our breath.

Movement can be anything from exercises that help you break a sweat to simply shaking – even laughter is a wonderful way to begin. By activating our bodies in natural and spontaneous ways, our brains are taught to welcome new ideas, thoughts and patterns of behaviour. Full-body shaking increases circulation, clears up built tension and is one of the most powerful ways to release blocked energy. We shake when our fight-or-flight stress response is activated, so by shaking with loving and healing intention, we train our survival brains that this change is wanted and welcome.

When we feel frustrated, blocked or stuck, we can release trapped emotions and reset through breath to inspire a flow of new energy. With each deep inhalation, we let new oxygen into the body, lungs and heart space, and as our shoulders drop with every extended exhalation, we let go of what is no longer serving us.

EFT TAPPING

An alternative treatment that helps alleviate stress, anxiety, PTSD or forms of fears that show up in the body is a powerful practice called emotional freedom technique, also known as EFT tapping. It draws upon the ancient

Chinese practice of acupuncture, where pathways (certain points on the body that energy travels through) are stimulated to improve the flow of energy. This involves tapping on nine different meridian points on the body to help move stuck or stagnant energy, essentially allowing the energy to move and be released. These can differ slightly, but most use the following: the heel of the hand, three points around the eyes (the eyebrows, temples and underneath the eyes), the area under the nose, the area below the lips, the collarbone, the underarm and the top of the head.

Start with establishing how intense your current feeling is towards a particular situation on a scale of one to ten. Let's say it's fear of taking action on your soul purpose path and making moves towards monetising your magic. For the first couple of rounds, partner the tapping with statements aligned to what you're feeling, and ending with 'I completely and fully love and accept myself'. So, in this example, it might be: 'Even though I am scared of taking action towards my soul purpose, I completely and fully love and accept myself' or 'Even though I have fear in what people will think when I start to monetise my magic, I completely and fully love and accept myself.' This is an intuitive and bespoke process using language that speaks to your soul. It allows for the emotional experience to be heard completely while holding a safe space for it with love and acceptance.

Then rate on the scale how intense your feeling is now towards that particular situation. The aim is for the intensity to decrease in order for you to move forward. Repeat this step as many times as you wish then move on to more empowering affirmations, such as: 'I know I am fully capable of taking action towards my soul purpose', 'I feel the fear and will do it anyway' or 'Monetising my magic is of service to the greatest good of this world'. Make sure that when you're saying these out loud you feel into the charge of the empowering affirmations. Again, repeat this as many times as you wish to dissolve those disempowering thoughts and emotions to a new empowering state of mind–body connection. Once complete, take three deep breaths, tuning into the body and gracing it with gratitude for all the energy moved and worked through.

All sorts of sensations are typical in an EFT tapping session, including tingling, crying and itching of the nose. After just one tapping session, you will be able to experience lower levels of stress and anxiety symptoms. Make sure to take sips of water throughout and after the session, too. This helps to reassure the body that it is safe and being taken care of while processing strong emotions.

LEANING INTO LOVE

There is nothing mushy about matters of the heart. In fact, research from the HeartMath Institute shows that the heart is the most powerful source of electromagnetic energy in the human body – stronger than that produced by the brain. This energy is projected throughout the body and radiates a 360-degree field beyond our physical skin, measuring around three to four feet (one metre). With every beat of the heart, there is a neurological stream of information broadcasting its message to every cell in your body, including the brain.

Emotion is the language of the heart. The rhythm of the heart is mirrored by our emotional states. Oxytocin, referred to as the 'love and trust' hormone, is manufactured in the heart. When we are in a state of harmony and the core feelings of love, compassion and appreciation are felt, oxytocin activates the parasympathetic nervous system ('rest and digest') and emits a frequency that others around us can feel. Choosing to alchemise each emotion to view it from an expansive lens of love will start to create heart–brain coherence. This extremely magnetic force field is in a state of oneness.

Dropping from our heads to our hearts will provide access to parts of our deeper selves. Understanding that we have the capacity to feel multiple emotions at the same time, we then choose to lean into love. The heart will send more neurological signals to the brain, affecting our thoughts, perception and emotional experiences. The heart is the source of emotional intelligence, and emotional energy is how we communicate with the natural order of the Universe.

When we are connected to our heart, we can hear the voice that says with quiet confidence: 'Breathe. You've got this.'

Soul Purpose Practice

Take two pages and split them into two columns. On the first page, label the left column 'Positive experience' and the right column 'Need that is satisfied'. Now list three to five positive experiences under the left column and the need that is satisfied under the right column.

For example, you may have experienced a time when you were upset with something your partner did but you were able to speak up openly and honestly about it, resulting in positive growth for your relationship. The need that is satisfied is feeling heard and being able to share your truth, allowing you to feel understood and loved.

On the next page, label the left column 'Negative experience' and the second column 'Need that is not satisfied'. Similarly, list three to five negative experiences under the left column and the need that is not satisfied under the right column.

After writing down your experiences, you will be able to identify the needs that feel most important to you to be fulfilled. Make changes or adjustments accordingly.

PART THREE

RE–
AW
AK

EN
ING

'Traveling is a brutality [...]
Nothing is yours except
the essential things: air, sleep,
dreams, sea, the sky – all things
tending towards the eternal
or what we imagine of it.'

CESARE PAVESE

CHAPTER — SEVEN

Manifestation map

WHAT STEPS WILL YOU TAKE TO GET THERE?

While I was living in London, I overheard a woman talking to her friend over the phone about a guy she was dating. She was discussing how they met, his personality, and continued on to say, 'I'm not really a manifestation person, but he's everything I've ever wanted.'

Maybe you think manifestation is a little too woo woo. Or maybe you're not completely convinced that this stuff actually 'works'. I understand, because I too was once sceptical. But at the same time, my intuition was calling me to explore deeper.

You may find that you already do certain manifestation practices in your life even if you don't think of them as manifestation. Maybe you've taken yourself to a place of feeling your fullest and most vibrant self, and a loving partner unexpectedly walked into your life. Maybe you've given yourself time and space to tap into creativity, and it turned into a profitable business venture. Or perhaps you have created vision boards purely for fun and aesthetics, unknowingly activating the reticular activating system in your brain which gave you a boost to take the next steps and call it into your reality.

We live in an energetic world. Everything on earth is made up of atoms, including you and me. Atoms are made of particles – more specifically, protons, neutrons and electrons. Protons and neutrons are located in the centre of the atom, making up the nucleus, with electrons surrounding the nucleus. Protons have a positive charge and electrons have a negative charge. What holds them together is an energy – a specific vibration or frequency. The only thing that makes a difference is the combination of atoms, which makes up the vibration or frequency. Our phones, objects, the human voice, emotions, colours ... they all emit a certain vibration and they are all unique.

In the Law of Attraction, like attracts like. Manifesting is the energetic response to what our own energy is putting out. We have the power to create any frequency within our brain and to transmit it. And whatever frequency we emit, we attract. This right here is the magnetic pull. The place of power in life where you don't chase, you attract, and all is drawn to you.

Manifestation is happening all the time, whether we are aware of it or not. It's like gravity, and cannot be switched on or off. We have a choice to either work with it or against it.

This is the power of manifestation and working with universal principles. We start becoming a co-creator of the reality we want to live. It may seem unrealistic or unattainable at first, but if there's an inner spark, it's within you to explore for a reason.

MANIFESTATION MYTHS

Let's clear the energy on some common manifestation myths.

MANIFESTATION MYTH 1
If I think it, it will happen

Many people who have watched the movie *The Secret*, which references the Universal Law of Attraction, may have gone on to think about a new car, romantic lover or winning the lottery – only to be disappointed when these things didn't manifest. Thoughts alone are very powerful, but this perspective often ignores the importance of the Law of Action: taking practical, inspired and aligned action steps, to develop skills and put in the necessary work to achieve the desired outcomes. While positive thinking and maintaining a focused mindset is beneficial in achieving your goals, it's unrealistic to expect that simply thinking something will automatically make it happen. Remember: small steps add up to a giant leap.

MANIFESTATION MYTH 2
I have to be positive all the time to manifest my desires

Feeling angry and sad or having a bad day doesn't mean we'll manifest bad things in our lives. While maintaining a positive mindset is valuable, the idea that we need to be positive 24/7 is unsustainable, unrealistic and, quite frankly, exhausting. As humans, we are born to experience and feel the full spectrum of emotions.

Life is a blend of ups and downs, light and dark, positive and negative experiences. Striving for a constant state of positivity creates an imbalanced perspective and unrealistic expectations. Embracing both aspects of life allows for a more holistic understanding that will lead to personal growth and authentic manifestation. This involves aligning our thoughts, beliefs, emotions and actions with our desires. Acknowledging and processing negative emotions can help us to gain clarity, release resistance and take inspired action towards our goals.

The truth is, the Universe will know if we're being genuine or not. It can sense our vibrational energy. The suppression of genuine emotions will do more harm than good. Embracing our authentic self means accepting the full range of emotions we experience. It's important to honour our emotions, whether positive or negative, and allow ourselves to feel and express them in a healthy manner. Suppressing negative emotions may create inner conflicts and prevent us from truly accepting and understanding ourselves. These feelings often provide hidden messages that, once understood at a deeper level, can work for us rather than against us.

MANIFESTATION MYTH 3
It's easier to manifest small things than big things

The size of what we want to manifest does not determine its ease or difficulty. Manifestation is ultimately a reflection of our beliefs, alignment and actions. Believing that it's easier to manifest small things can create limiting beliefs that will undermine our ability to manifest bigger desires. After all, perceptions will vary between individuals. One person may perceive one hundred dollars as spare change, while another may see it as a large sum of money. When we align ourselves with what we truly want, regardless of its size, we will create a fertile ground for manifestation to occur.

Manifestation is a skill that can be developed and strengthened through practice. By starting with smaller manifestations, we can gain confidence in our ability to manifest and refine our techniques. As we build our manifestation muscle, we will become more adept at aligning with and manifesting larger goals.

It is important to be patient and persistent. The process may involve overcoming challenges, which applies to manifestations of any scale. 'Bigger' things often require personal growth, expansion of our beliefs and stepping out of our comfort zone. These experiences can be transformative and enriching, helping us to develop new skills, gain confidence and discover our full potential. By adopting a mindset of possibility, we will be able to overcome limitations and resistance, and manifest the grandest visions that may have seemed impossible at first.

MANIFESTATION MYTH 4
Manifestation has no evidence

Although manifestation can often be thought of as a 'woo woo' spiritual practice, there has been much scientific research into the mind–body connection, showing the impact of thoughts, beliefs and emotions on our physical and mental wellbeing.

According to Albert Einstein and Thomas Edison, the most powerful transmitter of frequency is in the brain, and that frequency affects all matter in our reality. We can look to the research in neuroplasticity, the power of visualisation, mirror neurons and quantum physics for assurance, and learn to surrender and trust, as there is the element of faith in the manifestation process.

Masaru Emoto's work *The Hidden Messages in Water* demonstrates that the aesthetic properties of water changed when it was exposed to different words, phrases, pictures or music. The water exposed to positive and loving words and thoughts resulted in beautiful snowflake-like crystals being formed, while the water with negative words resulted in disfigured and polluted physical molecular formations. These were all captured with microscopic photography.

MANIFESTATION MYTH 5
Manifestation guarantees a specific outcome or desired result

Some people believe that manifestation guarantees the fulfilment of every desire. However, it is important to understand that manifestation is not a foolproof or one-size-fits-all system. Our thoughts and beliefs will influence our experiences, but external factors, circumstances and free will also play a significant role.

The Universe operates in its own mysterious ways, which is the beauty of it all. Factors beyond our control may need to align for the desired result to manifest. God may have a broader perspective and guide us on a different path that we are not aware of – one that is in better alignment with our soul's growth and happiness.

Manifestation is intricately connected to personal growth and evolution. Sometimes the process of manifesting a desire involves inner transformation and learning valuable lessons along the way. Be open to the idea that the journey itself may bring unexpected outcomes or lead us to something even more fulfilling than what we had initially desired. There are many roads to our destination. We just need to keep going.

What you desire may not manifest immediately. There may be other lessons or experiences that need to unfold first. There's a chance it won't work out exactly the way you think it will either. It may work out better than you imagined. I've found the best way to approach this is with an open mind, open heart and detachment from rigid expectations. Flexibility, trust in the process and a willingness to adapt will help to navigate the journey with more ease and greater peace of mind.

It's this, or something better.

What you desire may not
manifest immediately.
There may be other
lessons or experiences
that need to unfold first.
There's a chance it won't
work out exactly the way
you think it will either.
It may work out better
than you imagined.

MANIFESTING WITH INTENT

Thousands of individuals have now gone through my manifestation masterclass, which puts them into the driver's seat of their lives so they can manifest with intent. This is where I highlight that mindset and movement = manifestation.

To simplify the process, we can look to these five intentional steps (understanding that there are intricacies to also be aware of):

1. *Understand how the Universe works*

2. *Get crystal clear on the vision*

3. *Emotional embodiment*

4. *Inspired aligned action*

5. *Trust and surrender*

STEP 1
UNDERSTAND HOW THE UNIVERSE WORKS

Manifestation is not only about the Law of Attraction. To truly do anything with intention, we must first understand what we're working with – both internally and externally. The Law of Polarity states that everything in the Universe has an opposite that cannot exist without the other; this is necessary for balance. We can see this through good and bad, positive and negative, light and dark, masculine and feminine, yin and yang. Everything in any given situation is neutral – it's our individual perception that creates meaning behind it.

When the focus of a specific goal is only seen through a positive lens, you may self-sabotage even though you are certain you want it and feel capable of achieving it. Just like Carmen, there may be something that keeps stopping you that you can't quite put your finger on. This is because even though externally you are taking all the actions or saying all the affirmations, internally you have an energetic meter that seeks balance. As soon as you can recognise and accept both the positives and negatives for any given situation, you will feel safe to subconsciously move towards it and consciously take inspired aligned action without resistance.

For example:

More wealth and money can mean ...

+ I can buy more gifts for myself and loved ones

– I will have to pay more taxes

A loving partner can mean ...

+ I can share experiences with someone I adore

– I will have to make sacrifices and compromises

More career and business success can mean ...

+ I have a larger online audience to share my message

– I will be open to more criticism and hackers or haters

Try this: *list all the 'good' and 'bad' things about a particular goal. Open up and explore your willingness to accept both sides.*

STEP 2
GET CRYSTAL CLEAR ON THE VISION

If you don't know what it is you want, it will become more difficult to work with the Universe to make it happen. Start by getting clear on your soul desires and creating your destination of desire. There's no need to think about the *how* for now, only the *what*. When you can detach from the specificities, you release any blocks. This allows for limitless possibilities. Setting intentions will override any subconscious resistance that may come up along the way.

Those who have successfully manifested sometimes say they didn't have a vision before calling in their desires; however, what a vision allows for is the ability to feel the emotions of what it would and could feel like to live your desires.

Try this: *create a soul statement (similar to a mission statement, but less formal). Write down how your manifestation will serve and positively influence your life, and how it will serve and positively influence the greater good of all (powerful fuel for your Why, by the way). At the end, sign off with gratitude – 'This or something better'.*

STEP 3
EMOTIONAL EMBODIMENT

The language of the Universe is vibration and frequency. So if you want to intentionally co-create with the Universe then you've got to speak its language, right? This is exactly what emotional embodiment entails. If you want to manifest your desires faster, you need to step into the high vibration of feeling grateful, as if your desires are already occurring right now.

This isn't just about writing in your gratitude journal or doing a ten-minute meditation in the morning; it's taking that energy throughout your entire day and into the tiniest details from your morning rituals to meetings, and everything in between. Life loves a grateful heart.

The Law of Divine Oneness states that when you become one with your desire, you attract it. In other words, you don't manifest what you want, you manifest what you are. It's the feeling states within you that change your energy and frequency. It's *being until you become.*

What can end up happening when you are on the journey of personal development and self-growth is that positive affirmations are practised but are rejected by your subconscious. You find yourself saying a bunch of empty words when what you really need to do is to feel deeper. This can be difficult, as growing up you were likely taught to hide the way you actually feel. Were you ever told to stop crying when you were upset? Or to calm down when you were excited? We've been taught to deprive ourselves of feeling when the embodiment of emotions is key in manifestation.

Get clear on your desires and bring those emotions into the present moment through everyday activities. If you keep envisioning it to be so far away, it will always remain just one step ahead of you.

Once the emotional embodiment is underway, you will notice a shift in your energy, which is a great time to make a few commitments to yourself (more on this in Chapter 12).

Try this: *set reminders on your phone to check in with gratitude and feel into the emotions as if your desires are already happening.*

STEP 4
INSPIRED ALIGNED ACTION

The Law of Inspired Action states that action is necessary. I like to view action as the bridge between the spiritual realm and us here in the physical world. There are certain things we can't do that the spiritual realm can, and vice versa. It's inspired aligned action that activates the orchestration of synchronicities.

If you've been taking action already, this doesn't mean your manifestation will arrive faster. Part of the equation is also energy. Intention and energy are just as significant as the inspired aligned action itself. It's the process of consistently choosing to take these inspired aligned actions from an abundant state of being instead of a place of scarcity that makes an impactful difference. This is when we start to experience miracles in the form of being at the right place at the right time, meeting the right people and attracting opportunities. All forms of beautiful synchronicities.

Try this: *complete an action audit by carrying out the steps below.*

1. *Make a list of the actions you have been taking. (If you don't have any listed, this is a sign that more action is needed from your end. Take a moment to ask yourself: what do I feel called to do?)*

2. *Grab a highlighter and mark the actions that feel most aligned for you.*

3. *Replace the actions that you don't feel called to do (the unhighlighted ones) with those that feel more in alignment with you.*

4. *Go back to your highlighted actions and let more ideas flow from this space.*

STEP 5
TRUST AND SURRENDER

It is just as important to rest, not only to recharge but also to receive. Because when you rest, it signifies that you trust – you trust that it's all going to work out in your favour, you trust that there's a higher power guiding you in the direction towards success, you trust that the co-creation process is underway. To trust in a higher source is to trust in oneself. It's an act of surrender, which allows you true freedom. This freedom leads to leaps of faith that have a solid foundation, allowing you to live in the unknown with comfort and safety. This trust allows you to take the next step without the need to understand. It's rooted in curiosity over fear. No logic. No proof. Just faith in following what feels good. This is when you will start to see more signs and synchronicities happen. This is when you will start to get lucky.

Often our minds are fixated on the way we envision our goals and dreams happening. When we unclench our fists and find a way to surrender and trust, honouring the seasons of work and seasons of play, the ebb and flow, we can start to open up to the magic of the moment. There are infinite possibilities – ones we don't see, and others we can't just yet with the limitations of our human mind.

Try this: *ask for a sign.*

DETACHMENT

Detachment is not a means of giving up on your desires, dreams or goals; rather, it is not giving in to being solely defined by their accomplishment. Instead of clinging to specific outcomes and being fixated on the destination, it is a shift in focus to the satisfaction of what's alive in the present moment – the satisfaction of what is, instead of being hung up on what should be.

While it's great to have a plan, once you stop the need for control, you will be able to start receiving. This will lead you to experiences and outcomes far beyond what you could have imagined.

The control can make you feel safe. But when you catch yourself trying to control, get radically honest with why you are so attached and notice how it affects your energy. Then lean into a sense of curiosity as to what the Universe has in store for you, with a wide open embrace for surprises along the way.

Soul Purpose Practice

A Manifestation Map will give you an intentional overview of the manifestation process. A perspective of altitude, if you will. With this map, you will gain clarity and clear direction on where you currently are and where you are going (goals), identify and let go of potential road blocks (resistance), take practical action steps aligned on your path (whether big or small) and vibrate the frequency of gratitude to increase your magnetism. It will also serve as a reminder to lean into faith and trust the process, despite how hard it may feel at times.

Become comfortable with being in the unknown and open to infinite possibilities.

Jot down some brief notes on the map overleaf or transfer the map into your journal to create a more detailed overview.

HEALTH & WELLNESS

_____
_____
_____
_____
_____
_____

SELF & SPIRITUALITY

_____
_____
_____
_____
_____

CAREER & BUSINESS

_____
_____
_____
_____
_____

FUN & INSPIRATION

_____
_____
_____
_____
_____

LOVE & RELATIONSHIPS

_____
_____
_____
_____
_____

HOME

_____
_____
_____
_____
_____

WHERE I AM NOW
(MY CURRENT REALITY)

_____

_____

_____

WHAT I AM GRATEFUL FOR
(IN MY CURRENT REALITY)

_____

_____

_____

WHAT SMALL (OR BIG) ACTION
DO I FEEL CALLED TO DO NOW – OR NEXT?

FREQUENCY FIRST:
LEAPS OF FAITH

WHERE I AM NOW

WHAT I'M CHOOSING
TO LEAVE BEHIND

_____

_____

_____

WORDS I WILL REMIND
MYSELF, IF I GET STUCK

_____

_____

_____

CHAPTER — EIGHT

Your inner compass

WHO WILL YOU LET GUIDE THE WAY?

There is a magical superpower we all have, to make sure we are heading in the right direction – the guiding compass found within.

Our intuition.

The word intuition comes from the Latin *intueri*, which means 'to look within'. It is the ability to feel strongly guided from a place of inner knowing, without the need for proof, conscious reasoning or evidence to understand how. It trusts in the infinite realms and is often referred to as a 'gut feeling', 'instinct', or 'sixth sense'. This energy is magnetic and will bring us closer to our desires, should we choose to surrender to its feminine presence and follow what feels good.

Maybe you're working in a corporate job but long to fulfil your creative dreams, or you've built a successful business but wish to gracefully pivot into work that feels more meaningful. Maybe you want to know if you should go left or right on your drive home today, buy that apartment or wait for something better, meet that date, take that promotion or travel the world. Your intuition is a vital inner compass to what you're being called to or away from. Although it's often underrated and overlooked, it's one of the greatest tools you own for navigating soul-aligned success and a life that truly makes you feel connected and alive.

What does my intuition feel like?

What bodily sensations do I experience?

Intuition can manifest in various forms, like a sudden 'light bulb moment', a feeling of unease or warning, or a sense of alignment or resonance. You know those times when you knew something wasn't right, but you decided to go through with it anyway? Only to then disgruntledly say, 'I knew it!' and question 'Why didn't I listen?' That's when you've heard your intuition but dismissed it. We've all been there. We often ignore our inner compass to please others, because we haven't given ourselves the chance to tap into our intuition, learn to trust it and harness its superpower – or even see it as a superpower in the first place.

If something inside is telling you to take action – whether that be to leave a relationship (or be open to receiving a new one), move across the country, write a book, start a heart-led business, take a course – most often it's your intuition. It subconsciously knows your desires, but when you ignore it, you start to hear the voice of your ego mind: 'Who are you to do that?', 'You're too old', 'It's too late' or 'It's already been done before'.

The list can go on, if you let it. It can also stop, if you choose.

There are certain things in life that can only be seen, heard and felt when we slow down with awareness and attention. Intuition is one of them. When we can quieten our thinking mind, we're much better able to hear our inner voice of wisdom. Much like the essential tools of having a destination, map, and our *Why*, a key aspect to the voyage of soul-aligned success comes in the form of intuitive guidance. Whether we acknowledge it or not, we experience intuition every day.

This inner knowing comes easy for some and not so easy for others. The good news is that just like with any relationship in life, it's something that can be supported by getting to know our true self with conscious attention and focus. The bad news is that most of us either don't prioritise the time or even bother at all. Tell me, when was the last time you practised stillness in solitude? No music, no phone, no laptop, no notifications – no distractions. As social creatures, we spend plenty of time getting to know others but rarely do we carve out time to get to know ourselves. If we stop and slow down to become present, we can find the thread that connects us to an inner source of wisdom. The deeper we go and give ourselves that chance for connection, the more we're able to gather and instinctively understand what is of importance to us, and what isn't. Trusting and following the *what* without getting too caught up in the *how*.

SOUL SELF CHECK-IN

What are some ways I can meet myself in each moment?

THE FOUR CLAIRS

In the realm of the mysterious, there are four common clairs that we can become familiar with to receive information intuitively, and to fine-tune our connection to a deeper knowing:

1. *Clairvoyance*

2. *Clairaudience*

3. *Clairsentience*

4. *Claircognisance*

CLAIRVOYANCE
(CLEAR SEEING)

People with clairvoyance as a strong sense see or receive an inner vision that generally happens through our mind's eye. This can be through vivid dreams, colours, auras or creative expression. We are familiar with this gift through clairvoyants – individuals who view through a magical looking glass to relay information back to us – but clairvoyance is also seen in visionary entrepreneurs as they envision design trends before they become mainstream or create new ways of living through innovation. When we bring this back to our own everyday lives, we may experience 'clear seeing' if we catch ourselves saying things like 'I see what you mean' while in conversation with someone. Paying attention to our language can give us clues as to which clair is most prominent in our own intuition.

CLAIRAUDIENCE
(CLEAR HEARING)

This is the enchanting gift of hearing beyond what is audible to most people, as if the Universe is whispering into the ears of those blessed with this ability. This can be seen in music producers who effortlessly blend melodies and harmonies, producing captivating symphonies that touch souls. Or writers who hear words being spoken and quickly try to grab each one by writing it down before it passes by. This can even extend to the whispers of your own soul speaking, once acknowledged and brought to life.

CLAIRSENTIENCE
(CLEAR SENSING)

This is the most powerful sensitivity and involves perceiving or sensing information from people, places and different situations. This can look like walking into a room full of people and feeling that the vibe is 'off', or sensing that there has just been an argument. These qualities are within people who can listen with their heart and sense the unspoken words and emotions of those they are in conversation with. If you identify with being an empath like myself, you may relate to this clair. Many empaths have a connection to the clairsentience gift, feeling the emotional energies of others and having a heightened ability to absorb different emotional states. This connection to the world around you can make it hard to distinguish between what is yours and what belongs to others. It also has the power to ignite a spark of hope, to bring warmth to aching hearts and to build bridges of understanding.

CLAIRCOGNISANCE
(CLEAR KNOWING)

This is the wondrous gift of inner knowing, an intuitive understanding that surpasses logical reasoning. Those who possess this ability have a deep well of wisdom within them, seemingly accessing knowledge from a higher source. These are the inventors who we have seen through time conceiving groundbreaking ideas and inventions. They possess an innate ability to tap into the stream of consciousness, channelling innovation and transforming the world with their creative brilliance. With every breakthrough, they remind us that genius often arises from the realm of claircognisance. You may experience this by knowing something with full certainty without having any prior evidence. It can arrive as a sudden hit of clarity that drops in out of nowhere. You can't explain it but you just know.

These extraordinary abilities inspire a sense of wonder and awe. They remind us that there is more to life than what meets the eye and that the human spirit has the capacity to touch the extraordinary realms beyond our ordinary existence.

INTUITION VS FEAR

It is important and powerful to untangle the voice of fear and anxiety from our true inner voice of intuition. People who are attuned to their intuition experience lower levels of anxiety. But when anxiety does show up, they can identify what it is trying to tell them. It is understanding that it is not something that is wrong with them, it is their body communicating that something is wrong in their current circumstances. The more we let go of fears, the lighter we feel.

Following intuition comes down to self-trust. It requires radical honesty with oneself and allows for the intuitive whispers, rather than the fear-based ones, to come through.

Here are some subtle signs that show you're breaking self-trust:

◎   *You have a hard time making decisions.*

◎   *You compare yourself to others.*

◎   *You're not in touch with your feelings and emotions.*

◎   *You don't acknowledge or listen to your own needs or wants.*

◎   *You beat yourself up over your 'mistakes'.*

◎   *You tend to overanalyse or overthink.*

◎   *You're easily influenced by others.*

◎   *You downplay your success.*

What does fear look like to me?

Give it a name and a seat at the table.

While fear is contractive, the energy senses of intuition are expansive. Intuition tends to feel like a calm, inner knowing. It's relaxed and characterised by trust, knowing that if something doesn't work out, it's not the end of the world. While fear may have its logic and reasons for not wanting us to do something, intuition doesn't need a list of reasons. It is reason enough. With practice, we can learn to assess our intuitive experiences and identify when they are more likely to be right. We need the wisdom of both to be able to discern which path to follow.

In a world dominated by logic and reason, intuition defies conventional boundaries. It doesn't ask for proof or justification; it simply knows. Our logical mind likes to make plans and projections, yet the inner compass of intuition has a magnetic pull that's indescribable and felt deeply within the body. It's a reminder that sometimes the best answers lie beyond the spreadsheets and algorithms. That to listen to our inner voice is to honour our intuition's wisdom found within.

We all have bodily intelligence. Our brains, bodies and feelings are highly connected, and when we learn to tune in, we can start to unlock our intuition for decision-making. Making decisions from a state of equanimity is extremely powerful in determining whether we are acting from the ego mind or in alignment with our soul.

To practise this, take these steps:

1. *Write down your choices.*

2. *Write down the honest intention behind each choice – your* Why.

3. *Sit and observe your intentions and what feels most true for you and your values.*

4.   *Read it out loud and take notice of any bodily sensations: a lean in of the body or a spark that lights up your face. Alternatively, there may be a slump in the shoulders, a drop in the face or a feeling of dread.*

5.   *Meditate to clear any external noise and make room for your intuition and intentions that are in alignment.*

Logic should never be abandoned, but it should also never be taken as the one and only law for decision-making. Always making decisions from a place of strategy, structure and logical thinking removes from the equation the wisdom that is already inside of us that we are not listening to – and wouldn't it be wise to listen to the very urges of our soul's longing?

Try asking that to yourself and see what answers are revealed.

There is knowledge, and then there is knowing. Trust that.

Soul Purpose Practice

Carve out time in your day to meet yourself in your morning practice: meditation.

While I meditate every morning, tuning into intuition is accessible to us at any time of the day. To create space and practise feeling into your intuition in mini-moments, try these steps:

1. Breathe in the moment with three slow and deep inhalations.

2. Pause and sit in the stillness (wherever you are) with observation.

3. Question everything from a higher perspective; draw yourself out then up.

4. Notice sensations with a subtle visceral body check.

5. Align choices and actions with your values.

CHAPTER — NINE

Permission to fly

WHAT DO YOU NEED TO LET GO OF IN ORDER TO FLY?

Everyone thought we would always be together. *We* thought we would always be together. We were committed to growing old together, our families and dreams all intertwined, my best friend and lover all wrapped into one. Marriage, a house and kids were the next logical steps. And yet I felt empty inside. While externally everything was telling me to 'stay', something internally kept whispering 'go'. I spent months, years, trying to silence the inconvenience of this voice within me, but it never went away. It just got louder and louder until I finally chose to listen. That voice, spark, inner soul calling ...

It always deserves your attention.

Just when I convinced myself that I had found a way forward and was about to let go and take a leap of faith, I was pulled back. Just when I felt the courage to share how I was really feeling, something would stop me. It was much easier to push it aside and get on with being grateful for everything I had. But the ease was short-lived. In the long run, it only made it harder and more painful. Making no decision was still a decision to stay.

I listed my fears one by one in an effort to meet them in the moment, to try and make sense of them all.

- *I'm scared of what my family and friends will think.*

- *I don't want to hurt someone I deeply love and care about.*

- *I don't want to disappoint my mum.*

- *We've been together for so long, I can't give up now.*

- *I'm scared of being alone.*

- *I'm scared that no one will ever love me again.*

I look back and want to hug my courageous twenty-something heart. These fears felt so real in the moment. And they were. These fears offered a pathway for me to get closer to standing beside every frightened part of myself. This was the catalyst towards deeper healing that allowed me to honour my soul's calling, despite disappointing another. To befriend my fears and merge with the wholeness of who I am – who I was becoming.

During this time in my life, my mother said something to me that I will always remember. As I sat on the bedroom floor, my phone held to my ear, she said calmly yet firmly: 'Aubrey, you need to fly.'

Tears trickled down my cheeks. It was in that moment that I realised I was looking for permission. And so, I granted myself permission to let go of the guilt of breaking the heart of someone I deeply loved, and to leave a relationship with which I no longer felt aligned.

Is there a person (or people) I notice myself seeking permission from?

I gave myself permission to flourish into the person that my soul was calling me to be.

Most people are waiting for permission from someone else. For them to hand it over like a permission slip signed by your parents to go on the next school excursion. But the time may never come if you wait for someone else to tell you it's okay to be confident, follow your dreams, take time or simply step into becoming a new version of you.

Research shows that the average age of a cell within our body is seven years. The rate of renewal depends on where the cells are located and what they do, but the human body is constantly renewing itself. Just as nature changes around you, you change and grow, leaving the old behind and becoming a completely new being – a new you.

You evolve as you grow older and change interests or enter different life stages. If you feel the need to justify to others why you have changed and wish to grow, know that you get to choose. You get to experiment, change, try out new ways of thinking, speaking, dressing and being as much as you want. Otherwise, you'll always be left wondering. Change may deter people from you – let it, I say – but it will also attract the ones who are meant for you.

Own your story by taking a closer look at all the ways you may be holding yourself back from fear or judgement, or holding on to the person you used to be. To honour your soul is to own it. And to live a life that shows you what it really means to be alive, you must give yourself permission to be true to you.

Grant your own permission slip and sign it however your heart desires to do so.

Permission to follow the inner callings.

Permission to feel your deep feelings.

Permission to surrender to life's serendipitous unfoldings.

Permission to hold on to what feels right and let go of what no longer feels aligned.

Permission to do the things that light you up, just because, for it may lead to wonderful or not-so-wonderful unfoldings.

Permission to rest (guilt-free!).

Permission to experiment.

Permission to take time.

Permission to dream big.

Permission to take baby steps.

Permission to unapologetically express yourself.

Permission to love.

Permission to be, just as you are.

Permission to choose freedom.

SAM

FROM FEELING STUCK
TO FINDING FREEDOM IN SELF-EXPRESSION

Sam, a seasoned, multi-passionate entrepreneur, found herself feeling stuck. She was living as a van-lifer with her partner while travelling across America, and guided clients who wanted to take the same unconventional route of travelling while working online. She felt like she had outgrown the version of herself that had first begun the online business, but was struggling to communicate the new version of herself which was craving to come through.

While we initially worked together with the intention of bringing out Sam's unique story to the world, what we uncovered was so much more. Sam discovered that she was holding part of herself back to cater to the audience she had already built online, feeling that her authentic self would not resonate with her audience. In essence, she was waiting for permission.

Sam desired to express herself more authentically and in a heart-centred way, to genuinely grow without having to water down what she had to say, and to trust that the way she showed up would connect with her audience, so she gave herself permission to follow her soul's calling. Her reconnection with herself provided a strong foundation of trust, allowing her the freedom of self-expression to share more of her spirituality and how it has transformed her own life. Despite feeling fear that her story would deter people or not resonate, she took action anyway. The embodiment of her new, empowering core beliefs and freedom in self-expression magnetically drew an audience of resonance and allowed for soul-aligned success.

YOUR SOUL PURPOSE

Soul Purpose Practice

Write your very own permission slip, sign it and share it.
#soulpurposepractice

In order to move forward towards a life I love, I give myself permission to ...

_____

_____

_____

_____

_____

_____

_____

_____

_____

_____

_____

_____

_____

_____

PART FOUR

SER

VICE

'I slept and dreamt that life was joy. I awoke and saw that life was service. I acted and behold, service was joy.'

RABINDRANATH TAGORE

CHAPTER — TEN

The other side of the mountain

WHAT HABITS WILL BRING YOU CLOSER TO HOME?

Sitting on the edge of the summit, I gave myself a moment to catch my breath, ignoring the sweat on my back, my chapped lips and cramped feet. Nothing else mattered in this moment except nature's magic that lay right before my eyes – not just in front of me, but all around. A 360-degree view of rainbow mountains unfolding one after the other. Striped hues of pink, red, turquoise, lavender and gold making up the unique mineralogy of Montaña de Siete Colores in Peru.

'Is this real life?' I thought.

As I watched how the mountains met the clouds in the distance, my thoughts dissolved, as did my sense of self. A magnetic pull drew my eyes in to follow the boundless colours making up one rainbow mountain, before revealing another, then another, and another. Then there was me. Standing on top of the summit. Caught in a daydream of infinite possibilities.

I'm not sure how long I was in that daydream. At that moment, it was just me and the mountains. And it was there that I came to the realisation that it was my duty to give back to humanity. To be of humble service to the world with what life has shown me and the personal mountains I have overcome.

Without climbing the first mountain at Montaña de Siete Colores, I wouldn't have been greeted with a cascade of many more mountains, only visible at the summit. Without growing in a long-term relationship, I wouldn't have known how to cultivate courage that involved disappointing another in order to be true to myself and my soul's greatest callings. Without working nine-to-five in fashion, I wouldn't have heard the creative calling that lay within the confines of my heart, and to trust it; follow it. Without Charlotte, Sam, Carmen and Clara reaching the point of their upper limits, they would not have experienced the freedom, healing and bliss on the other side of their breakthroughs. All parts of the journey are meant to be. You are walking nobody else's path but your own.

By creating habits and spaces (both internally and in our external environment), we can cultivate the courage to bring us closer to home and support our new way of being. Let's start from the inside out.

WRITING AS RITUAL

By fostering a writing practice as ritual, we can start to break down barriers, beliefs, and any kind of resistance between ourselves and the path of our soul desires.

Gratitude journalling, stream of consciousness, scripting and reflective journalling help to promote inner peace upon self-reflection and transformation. Through consistency, the connection with our own intuition will deepen and strengthen. Journalling doesn't have to follow any specific structure, but writing prompts can help guide us in an overall direction. By committing to honesty, our journals may illuminate new directions we want to take, or bring awareness to habits or patterns that we want to work on shifting.

Write about an event that has happened (either good or bad) and the emotions and feelings attached to it. Describe how each of the emotions look, sound and feel to you. Feel free to draw them if that feels better for you. Remember, there are no rules!

MEDITATION

There are many common misconceptions about meditation. You don't need to be religious to meditate nor do you need to attend a silent retreat. It is also not an activity you do only once before suddenly becoming enlightened. Meditation is the practice of focus and awareness and it has many practical advantages, such as reducing stress, improving concentration, balancing the immune system and developing creative thinking.

Although meditation is a simple practice, this does not mean it is easy. Focusing our attention and awareness is a practice of observation – observing thoughts without judgement, and then letting them go. If you are just starting out, you can begin with a shorter timeframe then slowly build the mental capacity to sit and observe for longer.

DEEP BREATHING

From the moment we enter this world, we breathe in life. Breathing is something we do subconsciously, with our bodies and brains wired to inhale and exhale in both restful sleep and wakefulness. Breath bridges the gap between life and our conscious awareness of the present moment.

Breathwork is an active form of meditation. It is a practice of consciously and deliberately changing each breathing pattern. With every inhale we breathe in new oxygen that nourishes the mind and body, and with every exhale we release toxins. Knowing we can always come back to our breath, moment to moment, puts us more at ease to move through any situation with grace as we work on our inner calm and peace of mind.

Deep conscious breathing or belly breathing gets us out of shallow breathing from the chest and deeper into activating the parasympathetic nervous system. It drives us out of 'fight or flight' and makes the body feel safe, relaxed and calm. Practising deep conscious breathing can be done anywhere. To begin:

◎ *Sit or lie down in a comfortable position – ideally somewhere you will be uninterrupted.*

◎ *Keep your spine straight, relax your shoulders and sink into your body.*

◎ *Close your lips and lower your tongue from the roof of your mouth. This helps release tension in the jaw.*

◎ *Place one hand over your heart and the other on your stomach.*

◎ *Inhale through your nose for a count of four seconds, allowing the air to fill the lungs and travel deep into your abdomen.*

◎ *Exhale slowly for a count of eight seconds.*

◎ *Repeat three times, or until you feel a sense of calm.*

AFFIRMATIONS

Self-affirmations are positive statements repeatedly said to oneself, designed to encourage an abundant and optimistic mindset. I have had clients mention in the early stages of working together that they regularly practise positive affirmations, but they don't see or feel any changes. That's because there is a significant part to practising positive affirmations that is often overlooked: how we view ourselves and the world to begin with, which is governed from our belief systems formed in childhood.

According to research, self-affirmations create new neural pathways within the brain when people practise them consistently and they are in alignment with their core values. Repeating an arbitrary statement that isn't aligned with our own set of beliefs is not a worthwhile pursuit as our subconscious will reject it. Our subconscious needs to have resounding evidence that it can feel safe to shift and expand into growth.

Rather than beginning with affirmations such as 'I am rich' or 'I am confident', try the following:

◎   *I am the kind of person who ...*

◎   *I believe in myself as a person and I believe in all my capabilities.*

◎   *I trust in myself and I trust my intuition is always leading me in the right direction.*

◎   *I find safety within myself as I step with one foot in front of the other on my soul purpose path.*

◎   *I have come this far, and I am proud of myself. I will keep going in the direction ...*

CREATE A SPIRITUAL ALTAR

An altar can simply serve as a reminder to take time for self-care, solitude and serenity each day, or it can be used as a space to intentionally connect and call in guidance from spirit guides or our higher self. An altar can be as minimal or as extravagant as our heart desires. Intentionally dressing up an altar allows for our appreciation and gratitude to be showcased through our personal creative expression. We can allow for new energy to flow by changing or rearranging the items every now and again.

Follow these steps to create your spiritual altar, or your very own soul sanctuary.

1. *Intuitively decide on the location:* The location of your altar can be inside on a table or windowsill, or outside in a garden. Ideally, it will be located in a place where you will be able to sit quietly and in solitude. Set up your altar against a solid wall as a foundation that signifies strength. Clear any clutter to create expansiveness and uplift the spirits, allowing new opportunities to flow in.

2. *Cleanse the space:* Burning sage is a powerful ancient ritual for cleansing and purifying the energy of a physical space, object or ourselves. Indigenous communities have been using this sacred practice for thousands of years, and this should always be done with intention, respect and deep gratitude for those who have done it before us. Buying sage from an Indigenous company can be one way to directly support the origins of this practice. When sage is burned, it releases negative ions that increase levels of the mood chemical serotonin, clearing bacteria in the air, increasing the flow of oxygen to the brain, and relieving stress and boosting energy. The art of smudging is

traditionally done with an abalone shell and a feather by lighting the sage over the abalone shell, gently blowing it out and then fanning out the healing smoke with the feather.

3. *Set your intentions:* Take time to sit in stillness and set intentions for what you would like this space to be and how you will show up.

4. *Place your feature item followed by your arrangement of curated objects:* Work with the elements when you are curating your collection of items for the altar. Fire can be represented through a wax candle; the grounding nature of earth through flowers, rocks, crystals or gems; water in a simple glass can represent purity and healing energy; and wind from your favourite incense can be used in communication with divinity, a symbol of breath that equals life for the human form. Add photos of your ancestors, statues, totems, oracle and divination cards, books, or anything that is special and meaningful for you. Your current vision board, printed and framed, may also serve as inspiration.

5. *Activate your altar:* When you are happy with the final set-up and intentions, it's time to activate your altar with your first practice. Set the mood with solfeggio sounds, or light a candle or incense in complete silence. Prepare a warm beverage and allow space for yourself to tune into and align with what feels nourishing for your soul. Pull out your oracle cards for a personal reading and sit for a meditation that includes your intention, visions and connection back to self, angels, ancestors or spirit guides. This is your time and sacred space to feed your soul.

What habits can I start implementing that support my new way of being?

There's a certain homecoming we all long for after any grand voyage. These days, however, home isn't just defined to us as a single place. We can find home in a person too. Someone who will joyfully witness our every becoming, hold us through times of grief, celebrate our personal power and bring us back to the authentic version of our truth.

What if that person was *you*?

The you that has taken a step back from looking through the kaleidoscope world, to connect with your soul and inner purpose. For whatever it is that you see within something – someone – else is a reflection of you. The beauty you once saw in someone else, it's *you*. The bravery you felt in a friend, it's *you*. The strength you witnessed in a stranger, it's *you*. The confidence you admired in a child, it's *you*.

It's all you. It has always been you.

Welcome home

Where the darkness dances with the light.
Where the healing is a part of you already being whole.
Where everything else – *everyone else* – is just a bonus.

YOUR SOUL PURPOSE

Soul Purpose Practice

For twenty-one consecutive days, try journalling, meditation, breathwork, self-affirmations or showing up with devotion at your spiritual altar – whichever practice resonates with you.

Witness how it leads to transformation and lasting change.

Write down ideas for practices or rituals you'd like to explore.

_____
_____
_____
_____
_____
_____
_____
_____
_____
_____
_____
_____
_____

CHAPTER — ELEVEN

Purpose-driven work

HOW WILL YOU USE YOUR TALENTS AND SKILLS TO SERVE OTHERS?

Maybe you've been feeling it lately. An inner pull to offer your own contribution to the world through purpose-driven work. To share something with the world that fills you with joy and provides a sense of fulfilment in your own life.

Each and every one of us is unique by nature. The combination of our DNA showcases this. This means that we all have talents, experiences and perspectives to share that are unlike anyone else's. Whether your natural talents or skills lend themselves to areas such as teaching, coaching, healing or leading, you simply want to step more into alignment with what lights you up, or feel the visionary call for a journey into entrepreneurship – the move into more meaningful work is a path to follow.

A big part of what makes life feel purposeful is when we find a way to draw on our passions and strengths to serve others. To do more of what matters to us and do it in service to the world. Work becomes profoundly meaningful when we do something that we enjoy. Using entrepreneurship as a vessel to actualise one's purpose used to be part of everyday life. Our ancestors helped their communities with their particular strengths and exchanged their products and services for the value they received in return. Simply step into alignment with what lights you up and surround yourself with others on the same path, with the same purposeful energy. Doing so will expand your thinking and bring out the best in you and the visions you wish to become reality. This will lead you on the path towards more meaningful work.

Free yourself from your purpose needing to be solely one thing by finding a common thread throughout the gifts that you have to give to the world, and your inner sparks that make you feel alive. We are not here to live in isolation doing what we love, but to share it with others in service to the world.

How will I serve others through the combination of my passion, talents and strengths?

EVIE
FROM PASSION TO PURPOSE-DRIVEN WORK

While Evie was happy with where she was in her life, she knew she was meant for something more and wasn't afraid to go after it. After following her inner spark and passion for design, Evie already had the ideas, drive and action-taker energy to branch out into doing something on her own. There was a caveat: it needed to be a business that would fit into her life, not the other way around. Evie struggled to follow the strict cookie-cutter strategies that didn't resonate with what she wanted to create: an online business that reflected her values of freedom, creativity and connection. She wanted the freedom to create her own schedule (she loved working from home), do meaningful work with clients she enjoyed, and have a positive impact on the world.

Together, we worked on her self-belief that her desires were absolutely possible for her, and Evie did deep work in reconnecting with the relationship she had with herself. This connection helped Evie to create content that felt true to her style, which provided her with clarity in the value she offered and helped her to set pricing and packages, along with firm boundaries and strategies to scale. Evie developed a business model that was in alignment with her values and solidified the ideal clients she felt drawn to serve, including wellness practitioners, creative entrepreneurs and purpose-driven businesses. In doing so, Evie has been able to monetise her passion and skills in a way that works for her lifestyle.

Soul Purpose Practice

Consciously make an effort to surround yourself with others on the same path, with the same purposeful energy. This can be through online groups, masterminds, associations, courses or meet-ups, local communities and like-minded friends.

Where will you seek out your community?
Who do you hope to find?

_____

_____

_____

_____

_____

_____

_____

_____

_____

_____

_____

_____

_____

_____

CHAPTER — TWELVE

Setting resoulutions

WHAT COMMITMENTS WILL YOU HONOUR TO BE MORE TRUE TO YOUR SOUL?

As my thumbs tapped away on my phone keyboard, what was a typo has now become a ritual in setting re*soul*utions, and a fitting title for the final chapter of this book.

These re*soul*utions don't need to be accompanied by a clock striking twelve, or involve any kind of fireworks being lit (although I'm not opposed to lighting a candle to set the mood). Re*soul*utions can be written whenever you please, so long as they are intentional, in recognition of your wholeness, and in service to your soul. They are promises to yourself – a commitment to your soul.

Whenever there is a shift in my being I like to set re*soul*utions that include personal commitments. I then activate them through ceremony, and finally surrender and trust in the unfolding of:

◎   *where they will guide me*

◎   *what they will teach me*

◎   *who I will become along the way.*

Here's a look at a few of my own recent re*soul*utions:

- ◎   *I commit to always following my truth.*

- ◎   *I commit to taking inspired aligned action, messy inspired aligned action if need be – at least I know I am moving forward.*

- ◎   *I commit to progress over perfection.*

- ◎   *When I'm feeling overwhelmed or in doubt, I will remind myself that I AM capable.*

- ◎   *When I'm feeling resistance I'll dive deep and swim through.*

- ◎   *When I see myself overworking I will tell myself the truth that I AM enough and give myself permission to rest, knowing rest will allow me to be open to receive.*

You may be called to create re*soul*utions when you are going through a big life transition, or when you need realigning and want to consciously make the shift in energy. There's no wrong or right time.

From this wholeness, you can begin the cycle of discovery, healing, re-awakening, and being of service with new commitments and re*soul*utions, again and again. This time with more grace. The next time with more insight. The one after, with more inner peace. Each time revealing deeper layers into your awareness.

Discovering (and rediscovering) the joys you had as a child. Remembering your values as you follow each illumination. Healing parts of your wounded self, letting go of limiting beliefs and receiving messages from your emotions. Re-awakening to the empowered and magnetic version of yourself, unapologetically expressed and guided by your inner compass. Permission slip, signed and sealed with devotion. Cultivating courage to contribute through ways of service, even turning passion into purpose-driven work if you feel called to do so.

With each and every moment, you arrive. It is better to feel lost than to have never embarked on the journey; feeling lost may simply mean you are in discovery – trust you are on the way. From this place, you can see endings as transitions, and transitions as bridges to the next phase of growth. What makes it all the more worthwhile is infusing the journey with the same curiosity and excitement we had towards the world as children in unity with our destination of soul-aligned success as adults.

Journey first, destination second. Always. Following your inner sparks ignites your own expression of purpose and authentic personal power. You start to glow your brightest, and when you share your own flame the world lights up.

Your job is to answer the call. But first you must create the space to listen. To notice the nudges that reveal the path. When you get the sudden urge or pull, please don't push it aside or ignore it. For now you know it's your soul speaking.

It's never too late to begin. You are always right on time.

Over to you.

Soul Purpose Practice

I commit to ...

_____

_____

_____

_____

_____

_____

_____

_____

_____

_____

_____

_____

_____

_____

_____

_____

_____

_____

_____

FURTHER READING

Chapter Three: Signs and synchronicities

C G Jung, *Synchronicity: An acausal connecting principle*

Chapter Six: Emotional alchemy

Jill Bolte Taylor, *Whole Brain Living*

David R Hawkins, *Power vs Force: The hidden determinants of human behavior*

Rollin McCraty, *Science of the Heart, Volume 2: Exploring the role of the heart in human performance*

Bessel van der Kolk, *The Body Keeps the Score: Brain, mind and body in the healing of trauma*

Alison Wood Brooks, 'Get Excited: Reappraising pre-performance anxiety as excitement,' *Journal of Experimental Psychology: General* (2014): vol. 143, no. 3, 1144–1158

Chapter Seven: Manifestation map

Masaru Emoto, *The Hidden Messages in Water*

YOUR SOUL PURPOSE

ABOUT THE AUTHOR

Aubrey Daquinag is a certified life and success coach, internationally published travel and lifestyle photographer, content creator, and author of the book *Wander Love*. She has spent over a decade using solo travel as part of her spiritual journey and as a form of self-development. Her professional work has taken her around the world in partnership with tourism boards, airlines, lifestyle brands and leading publications including *Conde Nast Traveler*, Tourism Australia, Panasonic Lumix Cameras and Pinterest.

From travelling beautiful destinations in our outer world to exploring the intricacies of our inner worlds, Aubrey now helps leaders, busy professionals and successful business owners create more soul-aligned success by reconnecting them with their intuition, purpose and personal power.

Aubrey is formally accredited in neuro-linguistic programming (NLP), clinical hypnosis, emotional freedom technique (EFT tapping), life and success coaching, and meditation. Her content and written works are infused with empowering perspectives and ancient wisdom in a contemporary fashion for the modern day. She has over eleven years' experience in creative content marketing and strategy.

Aubrey has lived in Melbourne, London, on the road with one suitcase, and now resides in Sydney, Australia. She brings her creations to audiences across the globe to guide new transformational ways of living with an open mind and heart.

@theloveassembly / www.theloveassembly.com
@aubreymaeofficial / www.aubreymaeofficial.com

WITH LOVE AND THANKS

This book wouldn't be possible without community, spirit and all the souls I have had the pleasure of meeting in this lifetime, so far. My family, friends, husband, travellers on the road, ex-lovers, ex-bosses and colleagues. My deepest gratitude and thanks goes out to each and every one of you I have met, danced with and have had the honour of sharing big, brave and magical moments with. I cherish every experience and the lessons I have learned along the way in both my inner and outer world explorations.

Alice, Antonietta, Tahlia and the team at Hardie Grant Publishing, thank you for believing in my vision to bring these words, messages and book to life. To my editors Camha and Claire, what a pleasure it has been to work with you, thank you so much. I am incredibly grateful for the guidance and support.

To all my amazing clients who have allowed me into their life and opened up so courageously and authentically, you truly inspire me more than you will ever know. Thank you for the trust, honesty and genuine connection. It has been such an honour to witness your transformations as you step into and own your unique essence and personal power.

Thank you to those who joined behind the scenes as I worked through the messy middle, my clients inside of my secret book club – we made it! And, of course, *you*. Your willingness to grow, heal and embark on the journey to becoming closer to your true self – your *soul* self – makes my heart smile. Like, really big. I hope you continue to meet yourself in each and every present moment, follow the inner sparks of your soul's calling, and give yourself permission to live your truest and most authentic life. Wild, worthy and free. The world needs more of that.

AUTHOR'S NOTE

This book contains true stories from clients, family and friends; however, some names have been changed to protect their privacy. Many hours of research and studies have been completed and mentioned throughout the chapters, including accredited training, retreats, books, coaching programs and more.

Published in 2025 by Hardie Grant Books, an imprint of Hardie Grant Publishing

Hardie Grant Books (Melbourne)
Wurundjeri Country
Building 1, 658 Church Street
Richmond, Victoria 3121

Hardie Grant North America
2912 Telegraph Ave
Berkeley, California 94705

hardiegrant.com/books

Hardie Grant acknowledges the Traditional Owners of the Country on which we work, the Wurundjeri People of the Kulin Nation and the Gadigal People of the Eora Nation, and recognises their continuing connection to the land, waters and culture. We pay our respects to their Elders past and present.

A catalogue record for this book is available from the National Library of Australia

Your Soul Purpose
ISBN 978 1 74379 990 1

10 9 8 7 6 5 4 3 2 1

Publishers: Alice Hardie-Grant, Tahlia Anderson
Head of Editorial: Jasmin Chua
Project Editors: Antonietta Melideo, Claire Davis
Editor: Camha Pham
Creative Director: Kristin Thomas
Designer: Emily O'Neill
Typesetter: Celia Mance
Head of Production: Todd Rechner
Production Controller: Jessica Harvie

Colour reproduction by Splitting Image Colour Studio

Printed in China by Leo Paper Products LTD.

The paper this book is printed on is from FSC®-certified forests and other sources. FSC® promotes environmentally responsible, socially beneficial and economically viable management of the world's forests.